Combat Focus Shooting

Intuitive Shooting Fundamentals

Rob Pincus

Fifth printing 2007

ICE Publishing Company, Telluride, Colorado

Library of Congress Control Number: 2006949433

S.P.E.A.R. System™ is a registered Trademark of
Blauer Tactical Systems, Inc.

Human Weapon System™ is a registered Trademark of
The Direct Action Medical Network.

ISBN-10: 0-9791508-6-8
ISBN-13:978-0-9791508-6-9

Printed in the United States of America

Table of Contents

Foreword

Rich Lucibella
Publisher, S.W.A.T. Magazine

In his first book, Rob Pincus brings a refreshing and analytic perspective to critical factors of gun fighting. Rob makes a convincing argument in favor of a shooting system that may be heretical in classic, "front sight / press" circles. He does so, not to for notoriety or to name a cool sounding technique after himself; rather, because his own extensive experience as student and instructor have convinced him, and many others, that his training and techniques really work.

In addition to being an extraordinarily talented shooter and instructor, Pincus is the consummate student. This has been repeatedly demonstrated in his assignments, writing for S.W.A.T. Magazine. When Rob covers a school or course for S.W.A.T. he inevitably places at the top of his class and, often as not, is invited back in an Instructor role.

The Combat Focus system has really come together during Pincus' tenure as Director of Training at Valhalla Shooting Center in Colorado. In a short three years, this world class facility has filled up and been booked solid, not just by the average concealed carry student, but by an impressive array of LEO, Military and Exec Protection groups. To his credit, the Combat Focus training model has been adopted by several police agencies and he is currently involved in Instructor Development for Naval Special Warfare.

Over the last decade, I've watched Rob synthesize, test and refine this system in truly dynamic situations, with a wide variety of students. Owing in large part to his work with Tony Blauer and others, and his study of real world shootouts, Pincus makes a strong argument that we will not "fight the way we train" but that, in the initial moments of a violent encounter, we will all fall back on certain common, atavistic reactions. It is these natural reactions that the Combat Focus system seeks to harness and turn to our advantage.

It matters not whether you shoot Weaver, Isosceles, "Point" or "Front Sight". You need not reject your present system in order to benefit from Combat Focus. It represents an alternative shooting technique that all serious students need to explore with an open mind. Whether you walk away convinced that Pincus has significantly advanced the field of personal combat or not, does not matter; you will walk away a better shooter, no matter what "style" you choose or revert to after having read this book.

For several years, I've been telling people to expect great things from Rob, and this book proves that he's delivering on those expectations. While I have no doubt that Rob will continue to refine and evolve his techniques and training, his first book lays the foundation for everything that I expect to come after…and I expect much. In the training industry, this is a man to watch closely.

Rich Lucibella

Tony Blauer
Founder of The S.P.E.A.R.™ System

I first met Rob Pincus over the phone. He wanted to do a product review of my HIGH GEAR™ Impact Reduction Suit for *S.W.A.T. Magazine*. Rob had just returned from working at a tactical course in Florida. During the course, he was so invigorated by the performance of our HIGH GEAR™ during a day of force on force scenarios, he decided he had to do the review. This wasn't a 'product placement' angle, editor assignment or strategic collaboration... this was Rob's decision on his own; he wanted the training world to know about HIGH GEAR™. That's integrity. To me, that spoke volumes of his passion and desire to educate the police & military community.

After we spoke for the interview about the gear, Rob became intrigued with our research into behaviorally based combatives, startle-flinch conversion theory and isolation drills during force-on-force training, Rob wanted to experience it. This again impressed me: he wanted to learn more, see it and do it before writing about it. He didn't say 'Oh yah, I do that too', he said 'Can I do that too?' Rob really did want to expand his two arsenals: personal tools & teaching tools. Again: integrity.

Rob immediately attended a S.P.E.A.R. SYSTEM™ Instructor certification then a HIGH GEAR Scenario Instructor course and then our Personal Defense Readiness™ Instructor certification, all in quick succession.

What immediately struck me was Rob's uncanny ability to absorb the higher-level rationale of the system; the behavioral components that drives our research and training. Rob understood the 'substance' under the 'subject'.

As a student, Rob allowed himself to be guided. As a professional he impressed me equally by referencing and quoting our research in his classes and published articles.

That professionalism, the ability to remain the curious student and simultaneously galvanize it into a training process is what makes Rob's classes dynamic.

Rob has an uncanny ability to pick up the nuance that allows combat athletes to progress from being mere technicians to being true tactician. That shift requires a detached meta-cognitive appreciation of the application in context with the scenario. Many in the training community get stuck on the execution of the 'move' rather than the application during a scenario... and that's where Rob excels, his ability to create a scenario that draws the required skill from the student. As Rob says, he doesn't teach skills in isolation.

Some of you may be thinking, "Rob Pincus isn't some world famous competition shooter or alumni from a high-speed combat unit... why should you read his book?' Good question. Fans of the fight game often want people with the 'pedigree'. What's his background? Has he "seen the elephant?" The truth is that it doesn't matter. There are many great fighters who can't articulate what they sense, feel or understand and therefore they are of little value to the warrior student. If you're trying to improve you need a good coach, not a fighter. More important than his time in law enforcement and other endeavors, Rob Pincus loves to teach. That makes training with Rob (be it live or vicariously through his writing) compelling. This isn't a book full of war stories from Rob's various careers, it is a book designed to help you learn to survive your own. He is genuine about helping the student. Not only is Rob a natural coach, he's also a gifted writer. If communication were a martial art, Rob would be a black-belt. Masterful speaker - gifted writer... even if his concepts weren't cutting edge, the book is a damn good read.

Combat Focus Shooting isn't a re-hash or new label for some old methodology. Combat Focus brings innovative perspective to a deadly serious subject. It is the result of Rob's focus, his ability to focus on the metaphoric 'front sight' in the training world by blending his observations with lessons learned studying many of the world's more innovative products, elite warriors and fighting systems.

There are many ways to win a real fight, and as the famous expression goes, "In the end, its not who's right, it's who's left that matters". Combat Focus is one of the ways... This book is written with succinct clarity and provides fresh insights for training for a gunfight.

Stay safe,

Tony Blauer

President & CEO

Blauer Tactical Systems, Inc.

S.P.E.A.R. SYSTEM, HIGH GEAR PRODUCTS

www.blauertactical.com

"Learn like you will Live Forever,

Live like you will Die Tomorrow."

Mahatma Ghandi

Background And Overview

I say that Combat Focus™ Shooting wasn't developed, it was *recognized*. I say this because it was not as if I sat down one day to develop a new approach to shooting. Over the course of many years, in many roles, through countless experiences, observations, conversations, experiments, assumptions, theories, instructors, peers and, perhaps most importantly, students, the fundamentals of Combat Focus Shooting have become evident. As time goes on, the fundamentals may be further distilled, other principles identified or more efficient concepts formed. Combat Focus Shooting is an Intuitive Shooting Program designed to work as efficiently as possible with what the body does naturally during a dynamic critical incident. Empirical evidence tells us what is likely to happen at those times. We know that our goal is to end those incidents. Figuring out how to do that as efficiently as possible is what this program is all about.

The origins of my belief in intuitive shooting go way back. I was basically given free access to guns at a very young age and routinely went out shooting in the woods or the back yard at bottles, cans, paper targets, etc... I learned how to shoot with no formal training, looking at the targets.

When I started getting formal training (military, law enforcement, etc.) I first thought that maybe I had been wrong and that the "professionals" were going to teach me how to be a better shooter. What kept happening was that I was having to slow wayyyy down at close distances in order to do what they were describing (sight picture, front sight focus, whatever) in an attempt to attain tighter groups than seemed necessary. Totally artificial. I paid attention. I tried... I was a good student... I paid proper homage to the "professionals"... and eventually I realized that just because someone has been doing something (or whole groups of people) forever did not make it the best or even right way to do it.

Basically, for several more years, I tried to rationalize front sight shooting and intuitive shooting... not with much satisfaction. I came to the conclusion that two hits in one second that are six inches apart on target are infinitely better than two hits in three seconds that are in the same hole. Stopping the threat in one third the time makes you safe faster than perfect shots. Medical science seems to agree. At this point, understand that we have completely departed from any Target Shooting endeavors and are talking strictly defensive or dynamic recreational shooting.

With the ubiquitous use of surveillance and dash-board cameras recording critical incidents over the last decade, we are now able to see what actually happens during critical incidents. Combine this (largely, guys ducking and sticking the gun out in front of their faces while squeezing the trigger and looking at the threat) with quite a bit of behavioral research about what really happens when humans are scared (prompted and largely facilitated by my relationship with Tony Blauer and study of SPEAR System Research) and I realized that looking at the target while shooting was incredibly important to practice. We are hard-wired to look at a threat. The brain sees threats as a problem and wants to get all the information that it can in order to solve the problem... that means looking at the threat. If we practice our shooting looking at a 3mm wide piece of metal 24 inches in front of our faces instead of the threat, we will hesitate when our instinctive reaction and our trained response conflict with one another.

Oops... wait a minute... all the "best shooters in the world" use their sights or a red dot to win all the competitions... what's wrong

Combat Focus Shooting

with my theory? Nothing. Those targets are not shooting back, they are not causing any instinctive response from the brain and therefore, not causing a conflict of signals. Hence my philosophy that I do not teach techniques that were developed on a well-lit square range and proven in competition. Furthermore, those "best shooters" are professional athletes, not our "practice when they have to" worst case scenario students. Designing a survival shooting program based on what these competitors are doing does not make sense. Combat Focus Shooting is designed to work with what the body does naturally during a dynamic critical incident in the context of the student. This is not to say that competitive shooters have nothing to offer in the realm of defensive shooting. Without naming names, I've seen great examples of competitive shooters teaching armed professionals to be more dangerous to their enemies and I've seen some scary examples of successful competitive shooters offering gamesmanship as defense lessons and getting paid good money to do it. Suffice to say that if your instructor is teaching you how to set up your *fifth* spare magazine at the *proper* angle on your belt, you are probably dealing with an example of the latter. I've seen the same thing in the unarmed combatives world, where accomplished professionals fail miserably when they do not convey the important aspects of what they do in the context of the student. Royce Gracie is an example of the latter, an incredible competitive fighter who understands this principle very well. In his ground-fighting program for law enforcement, he is not teaching sport fighting, he takes the most appropriate response from his art for a given circumstance that an officer might find himself in and teaches the application in a realistic way for *Immediate Control or Evasion*, a concept that I have adopted for all unarmed combatives taught at The Valhalla Training Center. If you choose to go to an athlete for training, choose the right kind.

When in combat, the brain wants us to focus on the threat... the name was a no-brainer: Combat Focus. That said, let's be clear right away that Combat Focus Shooting is not a system based on never using the sights on your handgun! While there have been several other proponents of appropriate unsighted fire in the past, (Applegate, Rauch, Chiodo, etc.), too many people want to lump instructors into one category or another: The sighted vs. unsighted debate. As Ken Murray notes in *Training at the Speed of Life* (K. Murray, Armiger Publications, 2004), "The quest for the ultimate shooting technique has caused a pervasive rift in the fire-arms training community for years - Sighted Vs. Point Shooting." The truth is that Combat Focus Shooting is neither... it is about understanding the Balance of Speed & Precision and the principal of Combat Accuracy. A shot is Combat Accurate if it *Significantly effects the target's ability to present a lethal threat.* The Balance of the precision needed to achieve that goal (dictated by the target) and the speed with which a shooter can achieve that level of precision (their ability) is what determines whether the shooter will use their sights, use one hand or even attempt the shot at all (this is a product of their confidence in their ability). The more realistically that a shooter trains, the better the correlation between their confidence and their actual ability. The better the shooter understands their abilities under given circumstances, the better their cognitive response will be (i.e.- the more efficient it will be). The shooter that understands this will not be wasting time looking for his sights when he doesn't need them, but will use them when the need for precision dictates.

The evolution of teaching Combat Focus Shooting has come a long way since I've been running The Valhalla Training Center. I repeatedly see people who have never shot a gun before learn "Dynamic Shooting Techniques" to recognize and hit reactive and interactive targets (pop-outs, droppers, steel, etc) effectively while moving through a realistic 360 degree environment, in various lighting conditions with a lot of distraction, without using their sights after shooting less than 50 rounds EVER. For years I had been told that intuitive shooting was something one could only do if they shot thousands of rounds and practiced constantly. I now know empirically that this is not true. I have had hundreds of "guinea pigs" to test my theories on and most people (easily over 90%), regardless of shooting background, come out of their first or second scenario run convinced and confident in intuitive shooting. I have also found it entirely UNTRUE that you have to shoot 2″ groups in practice in order to hit an 8 inch target under stress... the trick is practicing in a more realistic way... it is the paradigm shift that Valhalla is part of: Train for the real world in the real world... or the closest safe facsimile.

The bio-mechanics of intuitive shooting are the same as with any other tool. I ask people who golf if they ever use a tape measure to confirm that their gripping the club the right distance over the ball... of course they say "no." I ask people if they hold a pen or pencil the same way every time they write... of course they say, "yes." By using a tool in a consistent manner, we don't have to think about how to use it, therefore we can use it more efficiently... similarly, if we use artificial gauges to confirm our consistency we might be more accurate, but it might not be practical to do so (i.e.- the tape measure for the golfer OR the sights on our pistols). Those analogies probably don't read as well as they sound in a class, but the point is that we need a consistent grip, a consistent presentation and a consistent trigger pull in order to be consistent in our shooting, not simple reliance on an artificial gauge.

Countless times, I have had students who are very good shooters who do not perform well when they first start shooting in a realistic dynamic environment. Their frustration becomes evident very quickly. In an interactive environment, it is easy to overcome this frustration, if the student is interested in becoming a better defensive shooter. At home, with this book in your hands, you might decide to experiment with some of the fundamental ideas herein. In fact, I hope you do, that is the point of writing the book. If you find yourself not able to shoot as accurately as you do using traditional mechanical shooting methods, don't get frustrated... everyone knows that this is the case. As you read through the book, you will come to an understanding of how intuitive shooting is about recognizing the appropriate need for accuracy and using your firearm efficiently to achieve it. The information in this book is designed to give you an understanding of why it works, how it works and the permission to try it. There are dozens of ways to shoot a gun and dozens of reasons to do so. Combat Focus Shooting is about shooting a gun defensively in a dynamic critical incident and doing so "as efficiently as possible."

So, the moral of the story is that if you give someone a tool and make them figure out how to use it effectively, they probably will. That's what happened when I was running around in the woods with a gun and no formal training. Combat Focus is just an affirmation and codification of that process. A new shooter in this program gets to do what I did at the age of 8 in a much safer and very comfortable setting and armed professionals or serious defensive shooting students get to "do what comes naturally" without feeling bad about it. Both groups tend to leave the experience with an increased understanding of their ability to react effectively and efficiently to a lethal threat.

Combat Focus Shooting is about efficiency, which requires EFFEC-TIVENESS first, but demands it as fast as possible and with the least amount of effort (physical and mental). Consistency in training, especially in the physical skills, leads to increased efficiency. Fundamental concepts that work under the largest percentage of circumstances possible increase efficiency. Realistic training under a variety of plausible circumstances increases efficiency. Integrity in your approach to that training and understanding of the fundamentals increases your ability to significantly effect your target's ability to present a lethal threat as efficiently as possible.

"Wisdom begins with wonder."

—Socrates

Warrior Expert Theory

According to educational researchers and psychologists, *Experts* respond to information in their specific areas differently than laymen. A intelligent person who knows very little about a topic can probably solve problems related to it by taking in information and processing it logically. An expert can see the same problem and *know* the solution. How does this work?

It is hard to define what it means to be an *expert*. According to Jeff Hawkins, the creator of the PalmPilot, the essence of expertness is the ability to, "through practice and repeated exposure,... recognize patterns that are more subtle than can be recognized by non-experts." (Hawkins, 2004). Identifying this ability is not very easy in most endeavors because measuring the speed of response is not always critical. There are some areas, however, that expertness has been studied and quantified.

Let's look at the example of chess. Most people are familiar with the rules of the game and can understand the basic problems involved, forming solutions to each new challenge as a game progresses. Usually, this means visualizing a series of moves and their potential consequences before committing to one move and then waiting for the next turn, trying to guess the opponent's move and contemplating reactions. While it is incredibly hard to quantify what it means to be an *expert* in any specific area, "the measurement of chess skill has been taken further than similar attempts with any other game, sport or competitive activity," according to Philip Ross, a contributing editor of Scientific American, "The results are ratings that predict the outcomes of games [at the professional level] with remarkable reliability" (Ross, 2006). Therefore, a Chess

Expert, is one who, after repeated exposure to the various possible conditions of the pieces of the board, can walk up to any game at any point and quickly make a decision about what move to make, without having to go step by step through a process of deductive or inductive reasoning. Having the patterns in ones head before seeing the problem, makes the decision making process faster. Studying this phenomenon has lead to a credible identification of *expertness*: The ability to use apperception to guide the decision making process, instead of logic or reason. Apperception is defined by Ross as "rapid, knowledge guided, perception" (Ross, 2006).

Malcolm Gladwell, in his book *Blink: The Power of Thinking without Thinking* (Gladwell, 2005), describes many research projects that have identified the practical applications of apperception in action. Think of *apperception* as the ability to use "what we know" automatically, without having to consciously process information first. (note: if you read the book, take Mr. Gladwell's theories about what he believes *lead* to the Diallo shooting incident in New York City in 1999 with a grain of salt... his description of what happened *during* the incident is probably accurate.)

If you are an Armed Professional, or if you are choosing to take your personal defense or that of those you care about seriously, you need to become a *Warrior Expert*. Start building the patterns of response to realistic attack now. Create templates in your head that might resemble plausible critical incidents that you could encounter. When you are shooting, don't just *shoot*.... picture yourself solving a problem... a lethal one. Tony Blauer created a drill for unarmed training in The S.P.E.A.R. System™ called "Emotional Climate Training." This drill has the student repeatedly expose himself to slow motion realistic attacks in order to create patterns of recognition and response.

The more information and experience that you can put in your brain through realistic training and practical thought about tactical problem solving, the closer you become to being a Warrior Expert. Attending a class, having a certificate on the wall or reading a book doesn't make you an expert warrior. Surviving a critical incident doesn't make you an expert warrior. Becoming a Warrior Expert is a constant process of gaining, evaluating and using information related to your chosen field of study.

I often say that I am not impressed by T-Shirts anymore.... I have seen examples of just about every cool tactical team I can think of make some big mistakes. I've seen people with "no experience" who were very dangerous individuals. Being a Warrior Expert is not about belonging to a club, shooting a certain type of gun or graduating from a school. Credentials do not equate to Ability.

If you ever have to engage in the use of tactical skills to survive a critical incident, you'll want to do it as efficiently as you can. The more you've thought about using those skills in a realistic way, the faster you'll respond and the faster you'll be safe. You'll want to *know* how to respond, not have to figure it out. The importance of training in a realistic way, in as realistic an environment as possible, preferably with interactive and reactive targets and/or good force-on-force role-players cannot be overstated.

Attending a class, having a certificate on the wall or reading a book doesn't make you a warrior. Surviving a critical incident doesn't make you a warrior. Becoming a Warrior Expert is a constant process of gaining, evaluating and using information related to your chosen field of study. I often say that I am not impressed by T-shirts anymore.... I have seen examples of just about every cool tactical team I can think of make some big mistakes. I've seen people with "no experience" who were very dangerous individuals. Being a Warrior Expert is not about belonging to a club, shooting a certain type of gun or graduating from a school. Credentials do not equate to ability.

If you ever have to engage in the use of tactical skills to survive a critical incident, you'll want to do it as efficiently as you can. The more you've thought about using those skills in a realistic way, the faster you'll respond and the faster you'll be safe. You'll want to know how to respond, not have to figure it out. The importance of training in a realistic way, in as realistic an environment as possible, preferably with interactive and reactive targets and/or good force-on-force role-players cannot be overstated. This book focuses primarily on efficient defensive shooting techniques, keep in mind that shooting is only a small part of the solution to a critical incident:

"The Athletic Ability to Draw Fast and Shoot Straight is not nearly as important as the ability to recognize a threat as early as possible and respond appropriately and efficiently utilizing the environment, training and tools available."

You will soon read about the concept of Combat Accuracy as a standard for marksmanship: "Any shot that significantly affects the target's ability to present a lethal threat." In the larger picture of tactical training, we should always be looking for ways to efficiently be Combat Effective: Take any action that significantly affects the target's ability to present a lethal threat." Being a Warrior Expert means recognizing what those actions are as quickly as possible.

Safety & Training Goals

Whenever we train with firearms, or in any tactical/defensive endeavor, we have an obligation to make sure that we are focused on achieving certain goals. For my staff and I at The Valhalla Training Center, there are three components that should be present in all of your training:

Safety

Comfort

Competency

While *safety* is always everyone's responsibility, the real obligation rests with the instructors or range officers that are overseeing the training. If you are out by yourself shooting at the dirt berm, *you* are your own instructor, of course. A huge part of safety is making sure that the value of the training significantly exceeds the risks involved in it. All firearms training has some risk, but to push the risk beyond a level that clearly goes beyond the benefits of any given drill or endeavor is foolish. If someone were to suggest to you that you should do some of your shooting without hearing protection, for example, because you won't be wearing it during a real critical incident, they would be foolish. We *know* that shooting without hearing protection damages your ears. There is no evidence to suggest that shooting without hearing protection during a critical incident, after training with it on, will cause a decrease in your effectiveness (in fact, the physiological phenomenon of *auditory exclusion* protects us from just such an occurrence). The same goes for all the "stand downrange and experience a gun

23

going off towards you," crap. Foolishness. If common sense isn't enough, every justification for how those drills are "controlled" and "done safely" are exactly the reasons that the claimed benefits do not outweigh the obvious risks.

Be sure that you have a standard set of range rules to guide the actions of you and your fellow shooters. What these rules are doesn't matter, as long as they have integrity and are followed. The most popular range rules haven't stopped accidents from happening, nor have they overcome acts of negligence. It isn't enough to say "they should've followed the rules."

Comfort is not a warrior word, but Comfort is incredibly important to the learning process. If you aren't comfortable, both physically and intellectually with a new skill, you are not going to be able to get really good at it. Whenever you are trying to acquire or refine a skill, you must try to understand and be comfortable with it and the concepts behind it. I tell my military students that SOPs (Standard Operating Procedures) are fine for the situations that they are designed for, but they need to understand the concepts and philosophies that underly them if they are going to be able to adapt and adjust those principles to every situation in which they may find themselves. Throughout this book there will be concepts, suggestions and techniques which you will want to incorporate into your defensive training. If you aren't comfortable with those concepts, send me an email and get clarification. I said that Safety was primarily the responsibility of the instructor.... well, Comfort is a two way street. The student must ask questions and voice concerns so that they can become comfortable with the material and let the instructor know where clarification is needed.

"Just another tool for your toolbox," is about my least favorite thing to hear from an instructor. It indicates to me that they are either not capable of or not interested in explaining the validity and principles behind the topic at hand. Ask questions, get answers, *get comfortable*, so that you can move on to the next step!

That next step is *Competency*. Once the information is provided in a thorough and articulate way, Competency becomes the responsibility of the student. As the reader of this book, the onus is now on you to become a more efficient and practical defensive pistol shooter. Consistency in your weapons handling, realistic practice and becoming comfortable with the concepts of Combat Focus Shooting are important parts of that process.

Keep in mind that *Competency* is a subjective term. If you think that some objective "qualification" test or performance in a competitive arena dictates that your are "good enough," your approach to Competency is flawed. Competency means getting as good as you can be and always trying to get better. How dangerous will your next lethal threat be? You need to become more dangerous than him so that you (and those you might care to protect) are safer.

"Numbers are Perfect, Infallible and Everlasting.

You Aren't."

Henry Rollins

Learning Opportunities

Alan Brosnan, Training Director for Olive Security Group, says that if you fire 1000 rounds at a target and hit 999 of then in the "x-ring," you only had one opportunity to learn that day. The fact is that you could have just been getting lucky 999 times... but if you can figure out why the one miss didn't hit, then you can improve your shooting.

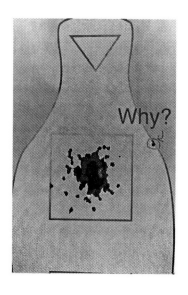

Be alert for any opportunity to improve!

If you shoot at a comfortable pace and get all of your hits during training, you might not be getting an accurate idea of your personal Balance of Speed & Precision. Worse than that, you might not be shooting as efficiently as you can. This is actually the most common thing I see with experienced shooters who take a Combat Focus Shooting Course.

After immersion in the Combat Focus Shooting system for almost a year as an instructor at The Valhalla Center, Brad Schuppan shared a drill with me that allowed us to encourage students to push their limits and see just how fast they could get Combat Accurate hits. This drill was one that he had seen used by another instructor as a trigger control drill in the past. The application in Combat Focus is a little different, as we address all the parts of shooting and usually end up making the point that our student's can make hits faster than they thought. This drill is among those described towards the end of this book, listed as the "Push Your Limit" drill.

When you are trying to get the best lap time on a driving track and while taking a corner you hear the tires squeal, you know you are losing traction (i.e.- being inefficient). The next time through that corner you have to do one of two things: Change your line or slow down. Eventually, you'll find the right line and you'll have no option but to slow down when you start sliding. Think of your grip, stance, trigger control and other technique factors as "the line." If you have the fundamentals right and you are still squealing the tires, you need to slow down, but if you never hear the tires squeal, you'll never how fast your lap time could be.

Try to make your training both realistic and varied. Realistic Training is not an objective statement. Just because you use reactive targets (such as steel droppers), three dimensional targets or train in a shoot-house of some kind does not mean that your training is realistic. You must try to make your training fit the context of your real world situations as much as possible. If you spend a significant amount of time everyday seated or driving and you never practice seated shooting, for example, your missing a huge opportunity to train realistically. Similarly, if you carry a small revolver, but find a large semi-auto easier and more fun to train with, you are preventing your training from being as realistic as possible.

Realistic training also means using your gear the way you will have it in the real world. If you keep a spare magazine in your coat pocket when you carry a defensive gun, but always practice with 4 spare magazines on your belt, you're training might still be very good, but it is not as real as it could be. If you carry your gun in fanny pack or purse for defense, but train from a holster "because everyone else does" there is a huge discrepancy between your range work and your real defensive training needs.

When you are training, make it as realistic as possible and try to push your limits. When you are shooting in a realistic context, see just how fast you can go.

"Anybody can be efficient (it isn't a question of talent)..."

Robert Greene, *The 33 Strategies of War* (2006)

Efficiency

Your efficiency level is an individual measurement. In Combat Focus Shooting, the underlying question to all of our skill sets is "Can I do that more efficiently?"

As noted earlier, Efficiency includes *effectiveness* in the definition. We need to accomplish a task, but we want to accomplish it with the minimal amount of energy, effort and time. For someone who is very athletic and who has practiced a lot with a particular weapon, a Critical Incident Reload may be completed in under 2 seconds, someone else may take 3 or 4 seconds to complete the same process. The truth is that without more information we cannot judge the efficiency of either person. The first person is certainly "fast," the second is clearly "slower." Those types of descriptions have nothing to do with efficiency. If the first person is rotating the gun so that the top of the slide is pointed to their weak side and "sling-shoting" the slide with the weak hand, they are clearly not being efficient and could get even faster. Conversely, the second person might be doing everything right and not be capable of going any faster.

Recently, I had a conversation with a newly certified Combat Focus Instructor about the difference between "efficient" and "easy." *Easy* is a subjective term, while *efficient* is an objective, quantifiable, term. One person may find something easy to do while another may find the same task difficult. Natural ability, amount of practice, comfort level and countless other factors go into the differences between *easy* and *difficult.* Whether or not the task they are trying to accomplish is *efficient,* however, can be judged objectively. How much energy is being used? How many extraneous steps, if any, are there in the process? Can it be done in less time (by both participants)? Don't make the mistake of thinking that your practice or familiarity or comfort with a certain process automatically makes it *efficient* just because you consider it *easy*.

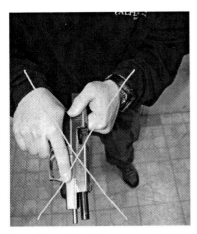 

Regardless of how fast you can do it, "sling-shoting" the slide is not the strongest nor most efficient way to get the slide into or out of battery. The overhand method, shown at right, is superior.

I often get asked questions like "How fast should I be able to get my gun out of the holster and on target?" or "How many shots should I be able to get on target in 1 second?" While these questions probably seem reasonable to most readers of this book, they are actually ridiculous unless they are put into a very specific context. What kind of holster? What type of gun? What is your target and how far away is it? What conditions are you shooting under? Without very specific information and having actually observed the person shooting, there is no way I could answer either question with any integrity.

I've stood within 15' of accomplished competition and demonstration shooter Jerry Miculek and watched him shoot six rounds out of a revolver, reload and fire six more into a pie-plate sized group at a reasonable combat distance in about 4 seconds. He's been recorded doing it significantly faster. This is done under controlled conditions, with a very specific firearm and ammunition, lots of practice and more than a fair amount of athletic ability. Give him the dirty 642 J frame that I usually carry in a pocket holster with Hydrashocks and no speed loaders and you won't see the same thing. Give me his gear and I wouldn't even come close to his level of performance.

Your shooting skills are your skills. Lack of practice, poor equipment choices, clumsiness, mental deficiency, techniques that add extraneous steps or don't work well with the body's natural responses to fear all work against you being fast. Efficiency is the part of the process of controlling these things. If you think slower than the guy next to you, don't train and are generally uncoordinated, you are not going to be the fastest shooter in the class. You don't have to make it worse on yourself by choosing poor equipment and techniques. Of course, the smartest, most coordinated person in the group is similarly hampered by poor gear and technique decisions.

It is more efficient to use a gun without a separately operated manual safety in a defensive situation. That certainly doesn't mean that you can't be "fast" with a single action automatic used properly. It certainly doesn't mean that you can't be efficient if your department has issued you a double action pistol, but told you that you have to carry it with the de-cocker in the "safe" position. In both cases, however, you could change the gear or the technique and be faster/more efficient.

Martial philosopher, Bruce Lee, in response to the question "How can I be a master fighter?" listed 5 components including the "mastering of economic mechanics" (Little, 1997). Regardless of how you express it, efficiency is imperative for you to maximize your skill level under any given set of circumstances and combative skills are no exception.

"The most important thing in training and practice is to keep it simple. This is will give you the proficiency to stay alive."

Walt Rauch, *Real World Survival* (1998)

Consistency

Consistency, at its simplest, means doing things the same way every time. Of course, as the saying goes: be careful what you practice. You need to identify the most efficient ways to complete any particular task under what is a plausible defensive or combat condition, and then you need to stick with it. Then, take a step or two back from the actual skill set you are working on to see if the bigger picture is consistent with other related skill sets. Once you have identified the most efficient way to reload from slide lock, you need to practice it in the same body position that you are likely to be shooting in if you want to be as consistent as possible. Next, make sure that you are doing it in a position that allows a presentation of the weapon back towards the threat that is consistent with your most common presentation (from the ready position, which, in turn, should be consistent with your presentation from the holster, etc.).

If any aspect of your tactical training is inconsistent with another aspect it will slow you down. During your training, always be looking for opportunities to become more efficient through greater consistency.

There will be times that you need to do things inconsistently. For example, if you are a soldier in a combat zone who spends a significant amount of time sitting in a vehicle between other duties, you might find it to be easier to carry your pistol on your chest while in the vehicle. Ultimately, this means training with the pistol in two positions, both your thigh and your chest. Consistency, however, needs to remain part of your training: always use the chest rig when seated and always switch to your thigh holster as soon as practically possible after exiting the vehicle. In both cases, you would still grip the pistol the same when at the beginning of the presentation sequence. If you were to be assigned to a low-profile mission and need to carry the same pistol on your hip, concealed, you would have a third variation. The requirements of carrying and using a gun in the real world do not always make consistency easy.

Consistency also means fewer choices, and having fewer choices means acting faster. One way that you can increase your consistency right away is to remove administrative weapons handling from your repertoire. When you load a gun, for example, regardless of the context: competition, target shooting, tactical training or any other endeavor, do it in the ready position, with your eyes off the gun. Not only will this increase your skill level, it will be more consistent with the worst case scenario: needing to reload during a dynamic critical incident. Now that you have chosen to use a pistol for defensive purposes, you are obligated to manipulate it as a weapon, not an abstract mechanical device. When you hold a gun, hold it in a good firing grip, even if it is locked open and you are just moving it from one part of the range to another. When you complete a string of fire or reload, don't just throw the gun back into the holster or "unload and show clear", come back to the ready position first and pause as if assessing the situation before continuing on.

The more consistent you are, the simpler and more efficient your training is going to be.

Run, Run Faster, Run as Fast as You Can Without Falling

Another way to introduce consistency in training is to not practice or teach things that you will have to "undue" later. Too often, people use the analogy of "crawl, walk, run". Thought about literally, the mechanics of crawling have little to do with the mechanics of walking. While walking and running are much closer to one another, a stop motion series of a man walking compared to a man running will show significant differences. Don't waste time with processes that aren't directly related to your end goal. (and make sure that you are thinking about the things you say on the range... someone might be listening and actually take you literally!)

"Reality exists as an objective absolute: facts are facts, independent of man's feelings, wishes, hopes or fears."

Ayn Rand

Working With What the Body Does Naturally

When we are suddenly scared or startled our bodies do a number of things automatically. These things are exclusively designed to protect us or to help us end the situation that is scaring us.

I strongly believe that through understanding how our bodies and brains work, we can more readily integrate our body's natural responses into our training and fighting plans. While some of this information may seem extraneous at times, those truly interested in making themselves more efficient warriors should consider this section a primer and seek out as much information as they can about the way their Human Weapon System™ works. See the Appendix provided by The Direct Action Medical Network for more information and suggested reading.

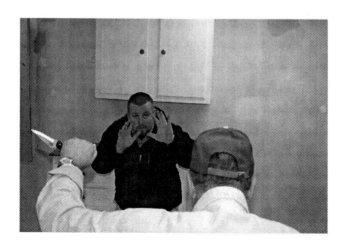

The Amygdala

There is no need to turn this book into a neuroscience text, but there may very well be a need to explain some of the basic concepts. The better you understand what is going to happen during your dynamic critical incident, the more practical and efficient you can make your training. Furthermore, by learning about how your brain and body work, you can ensure that the way you are training is going to be consistent with the way you'll be fighting.

Deep inside your brain is a structure know as the Amygdala. This structure is directly connected to the sensory regions of the brain. When information comes in it gets routed through the amygdala as well as going to the "higher" parts of our brain, the route to the amygdala is known as the "short path." According to *The Brain From Top to Bottom* (The Canadian Institute for Health Research, 2006),

"This pathway activates the amygdala which, through its central nucleus, generates emotional responses before any perceptual integration has even occurred and before the mind can form a complete representation of the stimulus."

At the same time, the information takes the "long path" through the cognitive portion of the brain to generate a more specific response. The "automatic" responses of the body to fear, startle and sudden close quarters attacks are generated by the amygdala before our conscious mind has *decided* to do anything.

"There has been no significant biological evolution, or change in human DNA, in the past ten thousand years" (Hawking, 1993). Given this fact, it has often bothered me that we have these same automatic reactions to both a rock thrown at our head and to a gun being pointed at us. We've had millions of years to develop automated survival responses to the reality that things flying through the air towards our brain are dangerous, but only a few hundred (at most) to acquire these responses to firearms. How does this happen? This question rattled around in the back of my brain for about 5 years until, very recently, I was reading The *Origin of Mind* (Geary, 2005) and decided that the author, Dr. David Geary, could probably help me to not only understand the process at work, but also how to explain it to you, my student. The latter was very important to the integrity of the system, because up to then, my answer was "I don't understand the science behind it, but it happens." While it did have integrity, it was not the greatest subject matter expert answer in the history of tactical training!

Dr. Geary is a professor in the Department of Psychology at the University of Missouri and I sincerely appreciated his taking the time to have an email conversation on this topic during October of 2006. At the end of this conversation, I expressed my hypothesis as this (Cognitive responses are referred to as "explicit" and the automated ones are referred to as "implicit."):

(from Rob Pincus, 10/16/06):

For my purposes, would it be accurate to say that after learning, the higher part of the brain is simply telling the Implicit system to react to the gun in the same way they react to something evolutionarily startling? So that the Explicit system is not suddenly sending separate signals for all of the Critical Incident Stress reactions, just sending one signal to "do that protective stuff" ?

The response I got was this:

(from David Geary, 10/16/06)

If the learned response is well trained, then the explicit system is no longer necessary. The reactions are governed by other parts of the brain and occur as if they where evolved, or at least close to this.

So, basically, when a startling stimulus goes down the long path through the conscious brain and the amygdala has not reacted automatically to it, because it is a learned threatening stimulus not an evolved one, the higher brain tells the amygdala to do its thing and the process is almost as automatic as when the rock is heading towards your brain. Note that, both in his book and in our conversation, Dr. Geary is very specific about the nature of the trained/learned stimulus. The more important it is to you (i.e.- the likelihood that the stimulus could kill you), the more likely that you can generate an automated response from the explicit part of your brain. For more on this, read *The Origin of Mind* and refer to the chart on page 168.

I have grouped the most relevant parts of the body's natural reactions into two sections, external and internal, for a reason. I have found that people relate much quicker to the former, as they can be observed easily in other people. The latter category, on the other hand, is experiential and has some components that are a little more esoteric. Furthermore, it is relatively easy to perceive the survival benefits of the external reactions to fear, while the internal ones may seem to be detrimental at first.

External: Orienting Towards the Threat

As soon as a shocking or threatening stimulus is presented to the brain, the brain starts trying to figure out what it is and how to stop it from hurting us. This is a good thing. Humans receive this threatening stimulus through one or more of the following systems: Visual, Aural or Tactile. Aural response is the fastest of the three, followed by visual and then tactile. The speed of subtle tactile reactions are also different throughout the body. While having a bullet pass through the hand or foot may elicit the same practical response, someone unexpectedly touching the back of your hand with a cold spoon will not elicit nearly the reaction that the same touch would on the side of your abdomen. Similarly, certain frequencies of sound elicit more of a response at any given volume than others. The speed of visual reactions are tied to the speed and proximity of movement, with faster/closer stimulus causing more immediate responses.

One important thing to keep in mind from this point forward is that the reactions that we are talking about are automated, not cognitive. If you get home and reach out to move a piece of glass bake-ware on the counter you pull your hand back immediately if it is hot and *then* you look over at the oven to see that it is on and pre-heating to 450 degrees, there-by deducing that someone had left it in the oven and recently removed it. If the withdrawal reflex from the hot glass were cognitive, you would instead look at the oven, deduce that the glass is probably hot enough to hurt your hand and then remove it. Obviously, the latter option, no matter how fast, would result in more damage to your skin. The body's survival reactions have all evolved like that, either to decrease damage to the body before the more contemplative parts of the process kick in to figure out what's going on or to speed up the process of figuring it out.

As soon as we hear, see or feel the threat, our brain focuses on learning more about it. The first part of the process is our orientation towards the threat. Humans are incredibly visually oriented. Our eyes are our primary means of gathering information. Even during our conversations, we key in on facial expressions and body language to help add context and meaning to the words we are hearing. When we are startled, our head, and soon thereafter, our bodies orient towards the threat for this very reason. Obviously, if we are seated or otherwise prevented from turning our bodies towards the threat, the head still orients the eyes towards the stimulus to try to identify the problem and figure out how to defeat, or avoid it.

Humans do not go toe to toe with natural predators and win. We survived to become the dominant species on the planet by out thinking and out maneuvering bears, cats, dogs and any other naturally stronger and better armed animal that we came across. The utilization of tools and shelter is part of this out thinking. Had we not observed the animals and their behavior quickly and accurately, we would have zigged when we should've zagged or failed to implement the right tool for defense or offense. The same is true for man to man combat. If you take away your ability to see your enemy, you'll have a hard time figuring out how to defeat him, let alone survive. With this in mind, we should try not to limit the amount of visual information we take in by closing one eye or focusing on a 3 millimeter wide piece of metal when we should be looking at the bad-guy, unless we absolutely *need* to.

External: Lowering our Center of Gravity

The next most important thing we do in response to a threat is lowering our center of gravity; generally, we bend our knees and bend forward at the waist. This response has been observed in just about every dash camera video and role-player stimulated startle response I have ever seen. The current war in Iraq, with the ubiquitous use of explosive devices combining with the constant presence of videographers, has given us countless scenes of men ducking reflexively in response to the explosions before consciously processing the information and reacting in a more effective way. In the event of an auditory stimulus from the rear, it actually takes effect before the subject has oriented his head towards the threat.

If you think about the human body, we have to lower our center of gravity to move. Even if you are going to try to jump straight up, you have to bend at the knees first. While it may be possible to propel yourself up a short distance by extending your foot rapidly down from the ankle, this is not a naturally occurring form of movement. Humans bend their knees and move the upper body at the waist to get from one place to another. Changing your location makes it harder to hurt you, hence the instant survival benefit. When we talk about the presentation of a firearm later in the book, we'll see how we can increase the odds of having the gun pointed in the right place even if the target is moving, but the odds are decidedly better if it is standing still. The principle is obviously the same for any other type of attack as well. It is easier to hit, stab, bite, kick, tackle or cut a person who is standing still. Lowering our center of gravity automatically puts the body in a position to move as soon as the brain decides where to move to. With this in mind, we should make sure that our stance is one that accepts this body position... any other training stance will condition us to adjust from this natural position which takes time and effort and is decidedly inefficient.

External: Hands in Front of Face

When we are reacting to a threat, we automatically bring our hands up to protect our head. Even if cognitive processing stops this motion and redirects it for defensive purposes, such as drawing a gun from a holster, the initial reaction can be observed. In the absence of a conscious action to increase our combative ability, and given enough time, our hands will end up oriented between our eyes and our threat.

The speed with which this happens is close enough to instant to be referred to as such. In review of 30 frame per second video of the startle flinch responses generated by simulated close quarters attacks, we generally see the hands move from the waist area to the face in between 6 and 8 frames (about 1/4 of a second!) when there is not cognitive redirection by the subject to draw his own gun at the recognition of the threat. The brain wants to put the hands in front of the face, specifically at eye level relative to the threat. For us to train with the gun at any other position is therefore counter intuitive. Contact shooting and extreme close quarters considerations aside, we want the gun in our line of sight towards the target.

Because of this phenomenon, in training we should initiate our draw sequence most often from a position that has our hands in front of our torso, between our waist and our line of sight.

Internal: Tunnel Vision

Of the internal factors that I will cover in this book, Tunnel Vision is the most important to understand. Physiologically, it is also the easiest to understand. The internal reactions to being startled can basically be attributed to changes in blood-flow. Fundamentally, blood is what brings energy to the various parts of the body. The more blood our brain sends to a particular part of the body, the more active it becomes and therefore the more work it gets done. In the case of tunnel vision, the increase of visual acuity in the center of our field of vision, the blood supply to our *cones* (one of the two types of receptors on the back of our eye, the other being *rods*), which are concentrated in the center of our eye. Note that I purposefully express this effect as an *increase* in our ability to gather information from the center of our field of vision. Too often, I've heard the phenomenon of tunnel vision expressed as a *loss* of peripheral vision. This is the same as saying that by putting more food in our refrigerator, we are decreasing the amount of air as opposed to increasing the amount of available nutrition. We have already covered the fact that the brain orients our head towards a threat, placing it in the center of our field of vision. Increasing our ability to gather information in this area is a significant increase in our ability to survive! The tactical considerations *after* the recognized threat has been defeated (the need to "break" from our tunnel vision and focus on that threat) is very real, but in the midst of an immediate conflict, tunnel vision is a powerful redistribution of energy that the brain does on purpose to make us more dangerous.

Internal: Tachypsychia

Technically, Tachypsychia is any perception of the distortion of time. When someone perceives a period of time as being shorter or longer than it actually is, it is because of Tachypsychia. In most critical incidents, the effect is a perception that time has slowed down, though this is not always the case. Unfortunately, we cannot hook a computer up to a persons brain and project their memories (much less their *current perception*) on a screen to see if they are collecting more detail in any given timeframe than at any other... we must rely on subjective testimony for much of the cited information in this area. There are many factors which effect this testimony in the real world. Careers, reputations, finances, family and many other things may hang in the balance of the difference between "It happened so fast, I don't remember anything," and "Everything went into slow motion, I recall the details vividly."

The overwhelming majority of responses in regards to the perception of time during the initial moments of fear, especially during incidents that had little or no predictability, indicate a perception that time slowed down during the incident.

Looking away from the lethal threat environment for a moment, the most common example of tachypsychia is probably the way we remember details of a traffic accident. When the deer runs out into the road or the other car blows through the red light, most people report vivid detail about the final portions of a second that occur before impact.

In the simplest terms, this is because the brain speeds up the processing of the information that comes in, especially from the eyes, during a dynamic critical incident. In these situations, you can think of your brain as a video camera that is recording at a higher rate of frames per second than normal.

Internal: Decrease in Fine Motor Control

The final automated response that I will address here is also clearly caused by a change in blood flow. During critical incidents, blood supply is decreased to the periphery of the body. Going back to our "blood = energy" analogy, those areas of the body, such as our fingers, are receiving proportionately less energy than they normally do, which equates to less control. For this reason, Combat Focus Shooting stresses using consistent large movements to present and align our firearm towards our threat and manipulate a firearm's controls whenever possible. While some fine motor skills, such as hitting the magazine release, are necessary for the operation of a firearm, by keeping the way we do these things as consistent as possible (including the position and timing at which we do them), they will be easier for us to accomplish even under a diminished capacity for fine motor control.

So What?

What does all this mean? Well, it means a lot. Too many people look at shooting as a mechanical process that occurs in isolation. Yes, you can be more *accurate* if you close one eye and focus on the front sight... in a vacuum. Yes, you can complete a reload faster with some guns by hitting the slide release to chamber a round... but only with some guns, under controlled conditions. Yes, you can hit your target standing up perfectly straight... but we know that you'll be crouching if you're startled, so shouldn't you practice that way?

Reality is Real. We cannot train hard or often enough to avoid tunnel vision (and we really shouldn't want to), we can't keep ourselves from lowering our center of gravity when we are startled, we can't miracle our hands directly to our firearm when someone pulls a knife on us in a dark alley. By accepting the reality of the conditions under which we will be fighting, we can train more realistically and be better prepared for our actual fight.

You may have heard people talk about how we are going to "fight like we train". Usually, this is supposed to mean that we have to train in a certain way so that, when we are in a real fight, we will react appropriately. The problem with this line of thought is that if we train hard or often enough, we can overcome our natural reactions. This simply *will not* happen. We need to *Train Like We Will Fight*. Our training needs to incorporate our likely context and the reactions that we know our bodies will have or we will *not be able to* fight like we trained.

Combat Focus Shooting is not about target shooting skills in isolation, it is about developing an efficient way to solve a very immediate problem which comes with a predictable set of factors.

"War is an art and as such is not susceptible

of explanation by fixed formula."

George Patton

Combat Accuracy

How many rounds will it take from your gun to stop a lethal threat?

Is it reasonable to expect a single round to stop a threat?

What is the goal each time you press the trigger?

When I ask these questions in a room full of "gun people," they usually focus on the last one and you usually get agreement at either "hit the target" or "stop the threat." Hitting the target is actually pretty good, but it is a target shooting concept and may not be enough in a survival situation. If your target was wearing hard body armor and you were shooting a .22, you may not have achieved anything by "hitting your target." Granted that is an extreme example, but we have to try to have as universally applicable a goal as possible each time we pull the trigger.

"Stop the threat" might sound good at first, but we know that this is not a reasonable expectation from a single bullet, especially a pistol bullet. Think about how you answered the second question at the top of this section.

A reasonable goal for any defensive shot is Combat Accuracy. Combat Accuracy is defined as "Any shot that Significantly affects the target's ability to present a lethal threat." A couple of examples:

A man pulls a knife out of his pocket and starts moving towards you from across the room, saying "I'm going to kill you!" You recognize the threat, move laterally while drawing your pistol, but instead of completing a proper presentation, you angle the gun out of the holster, start to sweep up and shoot early out of fear. The round goes into the threat's leg… he falls and drops the knife. Guess what? Your shot, which was textbook wrong in at least a couple of ways, was still Combat Accurate.

Now, picture the same guy, but this time, he is right next to you when he pulls out the knife and brings it immediately up towards your neck and knocks you down, pinning you to the floor. You block the stab with your hands, but realize that he is stronger than you and the knife continues to move towards your throat. As you continue to hamper the motion of the knife into your neck with your weak hand, you draw your pistol and feel the knife cutting slowly into you. At this point, that same shot in the leg may not significantly effect the target's ability to complete the driving of the knife into your throat… in fact, you may need to shoot the threat through the brain to get the action to stop in time.

These two examples are extremes in terms of the need for precision, but they are the ones I use in class to demonstrate the idea of how we are really only interested in the end result of any particular shot. Even if a shot misses the threat, but causes him to cower, drop his weapon, stop his assault and give up, the shot must be deemed Combat Accurate, according to the definition. This is hard for some people to get their heads around. The idea that a "hit" can do nothing and a "miss" can achieve a goal may be counter intuitive to tactically minded gun owners, but they are facts.

In a training mode, we have to have some target area on the paper, mannequin or steel that we are shooting. Looking at the body of empirical evidence from real critical incidents, we can say that most of the time a shot to the high center chest will significantly effect the target's ability to present a lethal threat. In training, that means that most of our shots should be directed towards this combat accurate area, understanding that any hit in this region is equal to any other and the more we can get in the shortest amount of time, the better. This is another important concept: One small knot of holes all touching one another in the center of a silhouette target probably just means that shooter was going too slow. Specialty targets (hostage situations, threats behind cover, etc) and scenario training can augment this focus on the high center chest for extreme situations like those described in the example above. By understanding Combat Accuracy, most shooters will be able to shoot faster by not overemphasizing concepts that come from target shooting and therefore prepare themselves to stop threats faster in a real incident.

How many rounds should we shoot? In the real world, it is vitally important to be constantly assessing the results of your shots on the threat. Luckily, most dynamic critical incidents occur at close ranges, where the brain's natural instinct to focus on the threat doesn't have to be fought against and hits can be achieved efficiently using good shooting fundamentals.

Understanding the actual goal of each round you are firing makes it clear that you need to be prepared to fire as many shots as it takes. Putting that concept into a practical setting and training realistically is incredibly important. When training, be sure to vary the number of rounds in your strings of fire. Don't get into a habit of shooting any specific number of rounds, or "double-taps." Picture a threat, and its cessation, and let that be what determines the number of rounds in a particular string.

If every round you fire during a critical incident is Combat Accurate, you will stop your threat more efficiently and, therefore, they will have less opportunity to hurt you or someone you care about.

"A man's got to know his limitations."

Harry Callahan, Magnum Force (1973)

The Balance of Speed & Precision

Of all the fundamental concepts within the Combat Focus Shooting Program, understanding the Balance of Speed & Precision is one of the most important to achieving maximum efficiency. This concept also helps to answer the ubiquitous "Sighted or Unsighted" question. The Balance of Speed & Precision might be the most important thing that a shooter should understand about training for the tactical use of a pistol.

First, a word problem:

If you are hitting a given target 90% of the time at 10 feet and you move back to 30 feet, what percentage of the time should you hit the target?

I ask this question to most of my shooting classes. I let the question hang for about 10-20 seconds while the students offer their responses. The most frequent responses are numbers between 60 and 80 percent. Almost always someone will eventually say "90%." Occasionally, someone will offer "100%" as an option.

Ultimately, the last answer is the correct one: If you pull the trigger, you should hit your target. As a practical exercise, however, the point of the question is that your ability to hit a given target should be consistent within reasonable parameters, regardless of the distance to the target. For the more nit-picky readers: 100 yard shooting with a pistol is not considered "reasonable parameters," but from 5' to 50' the differences in hit percentage for a given shooter of any skill level should be minimal. What is going to change is the amount of time and effort that any given shooter will have to apply to maintaining their hit percentage.

The fundamental rules are:

1. **The target dictates the need for precision.**

2. **The shooter's comfort/confidence with their ability to get the hit determines the speed with which the shot is taken (unless you are shooting out of fear).**

3. **The shooter's skill determines whether or not he gets the hit.**

If your training is more realistic and frequent, the correlation between your confidence and your actual ability will be higher. If you have only been target shooting and you do very well, you may be over confident in your actual defensive shooting ability. This is typically the case when an antiquated qualification system and training program leads a police officer to think of themselves as a "90% shooter" and they then achieve less than a 50% hit rate during a real critical incident.

Similarly, if you think you need to use the gun's sights to get combat accurate hits under all circumstances, you may be under confident in your ability to shoot unsighted at a target only a few feet from you and shoot slower than you could, thus extending the time that you are in danger.

Understanding these concepts and the way that they should influence your training is incredibly important to becoming more efficient. Let's look closer at the factors effecting the need for precision (Rule #1, above). Ultimately, there are 4 things that significantly affect the Balance of Speed & Precision:

1. Distance to Target
2. Size of Target
3. The Circumstances Under Which You Shoot
4. The Anticipation of the Need to Shoot.

Before looking at each factor individually, it is important to understand the concept of Deviation. Deviation is the amount of difference between where the muzzle of the firearm is pointed when the round exits the barrel and where you want it be pointed. Deviation is introduced by a variety of factors including trigger pull, anticipation of recoil, poor recoil management during multiple-shot strings, movement of the shooter and movement of the target. There is always going to be some amount of deviation, the amount of effort you need to put into controlling it is dictated by the need for precision of any given shot. Generally, the slower you go, the less deviation you will introduce. More specific ways to limit deviation will be covered later in the book.

Deviation

Think of deviation as a cone that extends out from the barrel of your gun in the direction the bullet is traveling. The greater the deviation, the larger the diameter of the cone at any given distance from the barrel. If the Cone of Deviation is larger than the target area at the location of the target, you risk missing. The trick is to keep the cone small enough at that distance so that it fits entirely within the target area. Match the target area precisely while maintaining good technique and you have found the perfect Balance of Speed & Precision.

As we discuss each of the four factors, keep in mind that we have to assume that everything else is equal when we talk about it's specific effect on the need for precision. If we try to discuss the effect of size differences between two targets moving at a different speed, things get confusing fast! Therefore, we will take each factor separately and define the effects in terms of deviation.

Target Size

The smaller the target, the less tolerance it has for deviation. A 10″ target any given distance will accept less deviation than a 30″ target.

Keep in mind that we are talking about *literal* target size, not the perceived change in size that comes from increased distance or an increased penalty for a miss.

Behaviorally, the size of a target can also effect the speed with which we shoot under Rule #2. Our confidence may be greater when we are shooting at a target that we perceive as being "big." By being aware of this fact, we can keep the correlation between confidence in our ability and our actually ability in check. In the same way, most shooters will try harder if they perceive the target as being "small." The fact is that this is an automatic behavioral version of the Balance of Speed & Precision principle...yet another example of Combat Focus Shooting working with what the body does naturally.

Distance to the Target

The further the target is away from the shooter, the more that the effects of deviation are magnified. If you go back to the original concept of deviation, the further away you get from the muzzle of your gun, the larger that Cone of Deviation is. Three degrees of deviation in any direction at 10 feet results in a potential miss from the intended point of impact of about 6 inches (a cone with a diameter of 1 foot). At 20 feet, the same deviation results in a cone with a diameter of 2 feet.

Of course, it is also important to realize that the distance from the shooter will also have behavioral ramifications on the Balance of Speed & Precision, similar to the size of the target.

The Circumstances Under Which You Shoot

This is a broad category because it represents the limitless variety of influences that come from the specific circumstances of your Critical Incident. Movement, lighting conditions, familiarity with your firearm, relation to recent training or past experiences, cover, concealment, other distractions, perceived penalty for a miss and any other influence you can think of combine to effect the speed with which you can take any given shot successfully. While most of these are self-explanatory, some deserve more attention.

Movement relates to the movement of the target, the movement of the shooter (see the section on stance for more on that), and/or the movement of the platform either of them are on (a car, boat, etc.).

The lighting conditions specific to your critical incident are often addressed in terms of target identification, but lighting can also have an effect on your confidence and/or your ability to assess the threat during the critical incident after recognition.

The perceived penalty for missing is incredibly important and is also a very hard factor to replicate in training. Take a typical training scenario where you have a threat target squared off to you at about 8 feet. You know you need to get Combat Accurate hits. How fast will you shoot if this threat is standing in front of a brick wall? What if the threat is standing in front of an auditorium full of grade school kids? That is what I am talking about when I say, "the perceived penalty for a miss." The behavioral component of this factor effecting the Balance of Speed & Precision can be observed even in competition, when someone "chokes" when the pressure is on after demonstrating the skill to make any given shot over and over again under other psychological conditions.

The Anticipation of the Need to Shoot also deserves some extra attention, as its importance may not be immediately obvious. What I am talking about is the likelihood in your mind that you will need to shoot *just prior* to your recognition of the need to shoot. If I walk out of my office in 10 minutes and find someone standing there with a machete saying he wants to kill me, it will take me longer to generate an appropriate response with a firearm to end the incident than if the same person called me and said that they would be at my office in 10 minutes to kill me with a machete. Of course, in the latter case, I probably wouldn't need to shoot because the would-be killer would find a locked door and hear police sirens shortly after showing up. Maybe some other examples are in order:

Picture a police officer with two subjects standing 15' in front of him outside of the scene of an armed robbery call. One subject is holding a bloody knife, the other has his hands at his side palms towards the officer. Which subject is the officer realistically going to be focusing on? In any version of the ready position, which subject is the officer's sidearm most likely to be trained on or oriented towards? How much faster will that officer shoot the knife wielding subject if he charges compared to recognizing that the other subject is pulling a gun from under his shirt and threatening the officer? This is the predictability factor that I am referring to. Certainly, the officer will recognize the attack and respond appropriately, but it will take him longer from the point of recognition for the subject he was not anticipating to shoot.

Have you ever been in a tree stand hunting and had a trophy animal walk into your range, but from a completely different angle than you were expecting? How much longer did it take to get that shot off compared to the time if the animal had come out from the direction you were anticipating and already had your rifle trained? Any shooter is going to respond faster if he is "hunting" or anticipating the need to shoot a given target than if he is surprised. Keep in mind that most square range training and practice is much closer to "hunting", so presentation times from a holster and other such "measurements" may not be very realistic.

Sighted or Unsighted?

I use a series of range drills (see the section towards the end of the book for some examples) to demonstrate the effects of all 4 factors on the Balance of Speed & Precision. During these drills, students will occasionally ask "when should I use my sights?". The answer is always, "I don't know", Understanding that the target and the circumstances dictate the need for precision and that every student's shooting ability is going to be different, it is impossible for an instructor to predict when a student *needs* to use their sights. We can say that at 5', shooters rarely need their sights to hit a realistic combative target… but, what if that target is a maniac holding your child in front of his chest? Combat Focus Shooting is an intuitive shooting program which includes the fact that the student must intuitively know when they need to use their sights. As the Balance of Speed & Precision tips further and further in the direction of precision it becomes more and more likely that the shooter should use their sights. Of course, with the speed component of any given shot reduced, using the sights and other mechanical shooting principles efficiently becomes more tenable.

The more often and realistically you train, the more intuitively you will recognize when you need to use your sights and the more confident you will become in the fact that you don't need them in many realistic dynamic shooting scenarios."

Speed is the Ultimate Control

If everything from your stance through your presentation through your grip to your trigger control and recoil management is perfect, the only other thing to influence control of deviation is the speed with which you take each shot. *You* have to slow down if you are not able to get the hits you need to get. Take a look at the three targets pictured in this section, each of which contains a 7 shot group. If we assume the shooter is a constant distance from this threat target and that all environmental factors are the same, we can say that the first target represents an over-emphasis on precision. The lack of speed might have cost this shooter his life.

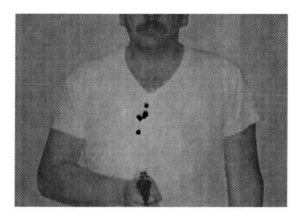

The second target shows a dramatic, and possibly fatal, lack of precision... quite possibly caused by an over-emphasis on speed.

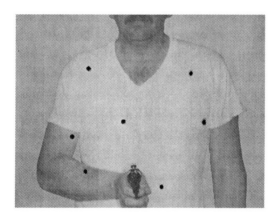

The third target represents a great Balance of Speed & Precision. While both Targets 1 & 3 represent *effective* shooting, the hits on Target 3 could be achieved much more *efficiently* (i.e.- in less time with less effort).

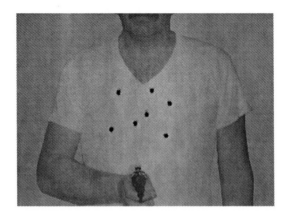

Once a student has experience shooting with an understanding of how the need for precision effects the speed with which they can shoot, they become more confident shooting under the variety of circumstances that exist in the real world. All shooting is a Balance of Speed & Precision. Given a very low requirement for speed, shooters can achieve excellent accuracy on any reasonable target with mechanical shooting skills, but combative (or defensive) shooting most often carries a very high requirement for speed and that means establishing the goal of EFFICIENCY in our shooting, not just effectiveness. The confidence that comes from understanding the Balance of Speed & Precision will make you more efficient... and that means safer. The sooner that you can end a critical incident, the sooner you are safe.

Stance & Movement

Think of stance as a matter of convenience. It is not necessary to be in any particular stance to get combat accurate hits. If you keep the relationship between your gun and your head consistent, the rest of your body can be however it ends up. Lying down, sitting down, turned around, upside down... it doesn't matter.

That said, there are some distinct advantages to being in a good weight forward, squared off to the target stance while shooting, especially when it comes to efficient presentation and recoil management. And, or course, we want our stance to work well with what the body does naturally during a critical incident.

In training, it is important to practice shooting from positions that you are likely to be in during your critical incident. If you spend 90% of your day seated, but you've never shot from a seated position, your training is lacking. Most of us shoot standing up. If you go to any given range on a Saturday afternoon, you'll probably see a dozen different stances; straight up, leaning forward, leaning backwards, crouched, bladed, squared off and various combinations of those options.

After having read the section on what the body does naturally in reaction to a threat earlier in the book, you should be able to predict that I am going to recommend that you be squared off to the target (oriented towards the threat) and have a lowered center of gravity when you are practicing your defensive shooting. To do anything else would be working against your body's natural position. Add to this the idea of extending your arms out in from of your face towards the threat and the need for good recoil management for rapid follow-up shots and you will find a need to have your weight forward towards the target, behind the gun.

Note the position of the shoulders out in front of the hips for better balance

The recommended Combat Focus Shooting Stance is very similar to what Wes Doss, in his book *Train to Win*, refers to as the "forward stance" (Doss, 2003). It starts with the feet equal distances from the target, which squares the hips towards the threat, the knees are bent in accordance with the body's lowering of the center of gravity. The upper body is bent forward at the waist, placing the shoulders above the knees or toes (not the hips!). The shoulders are also squared towards the target. This stance is the best combination of being athletically neutral, providing a good support for recoil management and presentation/retention of the weapon and working with what the body does naturally during a critical incident.

By keeping your feet equidistant from the target, you will be training in the most neutral position possible and not creating a dependence on having one foot or the other forward. this position gives you the greatest range of motion and ability to respond in a 360 degree world.

Note that the stance should not change from the ready position
to the actual shooting position.

Keep in mind that, in training, once you are in your combative
stance, you should remain in it throughout your training iteration.
Whether you are drawing your weapon from a holster, assessing
the environment from the ready position or actually shooting,
your stance should not be affected.

In training, a great way to get into this stance at the command to
fire or upon *recognition* of the threat, is to make a quick lateral
movement. From a tactical standpoint, it is a good idea to get
offline from the attack anyway. With movement comes a lowering
of the center of gravity. This movement should be quick and take
no longer than the time it takes to present your weapon to the
target (from the ready position or the holster). The movement

itself should be about one body width. The tactical application of *Lateral Movement* will be covered in the next book in this series.

It is important to note that movement should stop when we start shooting for maximum efficiency. While we often think of the movement of the target when you picture a combative incident, we need to take a long look at our "moving & shooting" options. Often, especially with my military special operations students, I see shooters who want to move while they are shooting, especially at close distances. Almost without exception, the shooters shoot noticeably slower and with significantly more deviation than they do when they are standing still. The imperative question is how much safer does moving make you? If we look at the speed with which most people move & shoot, which is relatively slow, and compare the success that most people have at hitting targets moving at similar speeds, the answer is "Not Much." I am not aware of any significant research in this area, but I can tell you from observation that I don't believe the net effect of trying to shoot & move at the same time is a positive one for you in a defensive situation. Consider this: If you are 10% safer by moving while shooting, but it takes you 20% longer to fire a given string of fire and it is 20% less Combat Accurate, you end up being exposed to danger significantly longer than if you just stopped and shot. Placing emphasis on ending the conflict as quickly as possible is paramount to surviving that incident.

The High-Compressed Ready Position

In the search for consistency and efficiency in every area of weapons handling and combative pistol use, the ready position may be the most debated and radically different specific part from one instructor to the next. While there are certain positions that offer isolated benefits in extreme circumstances, Combat Focus is about addressing the most common critical incident problems for the largest number of people. In pointing out the strengths of The High Compressed Ready Position, the shortfalls of other positions will be evident. That is not to say that they don't have their own advantages in specific cases, but I don't believe that any other position is as universally beneficial.

The High Compressed Ready Position is one that brings the gun in close to the chest, with the muzzle oriented below the line of sight,

the elbows tucked at the shooter's side and the shoulders, hips and feet oriented towards the front. From this position, the shooter can easily reload, clear a malfunction, assess his environment, present the weapon towards the threat, protect the weapon from being grabbed and move it into an extreme close quarters shooting position or do just about anything else that one might need to do during a dynamic critical incident with the most consistency and strength.

Close to the Chest

This means very specifically, the *chest*, not the belly. This is the "high" part of the High Compressed Ready. By keeping the gun up high in front of the body, you maintain more strength (arms bent, rather than extended) and control (it is harder for someone to reach the gun when it is tucked against the chest). As you will see in the next section, it is also easier to present the gun consistently and efficiently if the gun is held high in front of the body.

Keeping the gun close to your chest also keeps it out of your field of vision, allowing you to assess the environment around you more easily, including anyone lying on the ground in front of you, as you are moving through a critical incident or other tactical situation.

Muzzle Down

Keeping the muzzle down is, at some levels, a safety issue. In training, as noted above, this is a very real concern. Luckily for us, it also makes a great deal of sense tactically and when considering an economy of motion. The "worst case scenario" for needing to use a handgun when we have it with us is that it is in the holster when we recognize the threat. In almost every case, that means that the muzzle will be pointed down. In most recommended carry positions, the handgun will be coming *through* the area of the High Compressed Ready before it is presented towards the target. As the firearm reaches that point, the muzzle will either be pointed straight out towards the threat, or be rotating into a position that orients the muzzle in that direction. Having the muzzle pointed up in the ready position means that our presentation from the ready and presentation from the holster would be inconsistent. That is bad.

Next, let's consider any weapons handling function that we might want to engage in while at the ready position. I recommend manually manipulating the slide by reaching the weak hand over the slide, behind the ejection port whenever it is necessary to get the gun into or out of battery. Doing this with the muzzle pointed up is much harder and usually requires the gun to be pushed out from the body, resulting in more of the aforementioned inconsistency when it comes time to present the weapon towards the threat.

The last major endorsement of the muzzle down position comes in the area of retention and extreme close quarters shooting. If someone catches you off-guard and grabs your firearm with the muzzle oriented in an upward position, you will have to rely on your strength and technique to get the gun oriented into a position from which you could use it against your threat. If the muzzle is oriented down, it is much more likely to be oriented towards some part of the threat's body, regardless of their relative strength.

Elbows at Your Side

By keeping your elbows tucked into your side, you create more of a barrier from an attempt to grab your gun from outside of your field of vision. Think back to the section on "What the body does Naturally." During a dynamic critical incident, you will be intensely focused on the center of your field of vision, where your acuity has been increased physiologically and your attention is focused behaviorally, so having your elbows at your side can help to protect it from being grabbed from someone in your periphery. You may also recall that one of the ways that your body gathers information about an attack is through touch... consider your elbows and upper arms to be like whiskers in this position, telling your brain about an attack before you can see it coming. Should that attack be against your torso and not a gun-grab, having your arms here will also protect the ribs and abdomen much more than other ready positions.

With your elbows in this position, you are also ensured to be consistently able to extend the gun out into a shooting position; not risk swinging the gun up from a straight arm ready.

Lastly, this position offers very little fatigue, as you can actually be taking up some of the weight of the gun through your forearms on your midsection, body armor or other gear.

Orientation Towards the Front

By keeping everything oriented along your field of vision, you will be able to respond to threats identified efficiently. You are also less likely to have someone grab your gun from outside this field of vision or to bump your gun into something while you move or present it towards a threat. Bladed positions relative to your *expected* threat angle inevitably expose the firearm needlessly to attack from other angles or result in the necessity to reposition yourself to respond to threats to the weak side or end up swinging the gun towards a target that was identified laterally.

Presentation from the Ready Position

The presentation of the firearm towards the threat is one of the most often flawed parts of an experienced shooter's program. In actuality, it should be the simplest. Efficiency is our buzzword and, in this case, that again means economy of motion. How do we get the gun into a firing position as fast as we can? We want to get the gun into a position that is *in and parallel with* our line of sight. We also want both of our arms to be at full extension (assuming a two handed grip).

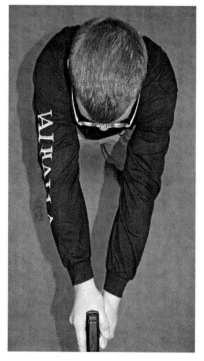

If the gun comes out of the holster or from the high compressed ready position, the muzzle starts pointing lower than our line of sight to the target, so right off the bat we know that if the muzzle ever points *above* this line it is because of extraneous motion.

Next, let's look at the way that the brain controls our muscles. The actual presentation of the firearm from either the holster or the ready position is the single biggest movement that is going to be performed during the shooting portion of most critical incidents. With this in mind, we need to keep it as efficient as possible. For this reason, and several others, we are going to want to extend our arms all the way out during the presentation. If our brain has to start *and* stop the movement of the gun, we are doubling the mental effort in this part of the process. By sending one message, "out!", our brain is less cluttered than it would be if we were doing two different things with our arms, or if we were trying to hit an arbitrary position between having our arms against our body and having them fully extended.

It is very important at this point to understand what is meant by "in and parallel with the line of sight." If you picture a firearm pointed towards a target in front of a shooter, but at their hip, it is entirely possible to get the firearm parallel with our line of sight, but it is clearly not *in* it. Similarly, if the gun is in our line of sight, but canted offline, it is not going to be consistently aligned properly with the target either. It is simple enough to get the gun in the right position eventually, but we must get it there as efficiently as possible. Think for a moment about the way the human shoulders and arms are built and move. If we fully extend the gun out in front of us, but at an angle towards the ground and *then* rotate the gun into the proper position from the shoulder, we need to send a message to the muscles to stop the movement as we reach the right spot. In this case, we need to rely on muscle control to stop the upward momentum of the gun. Obviously, this is not an efficient way to get the firearm into the proper shooting position. It is a much better idea to use the way our body is built to stop the gun's movement for us. This means that we need to get the gun in and parallel with our line of sight *before* our arms fully are extended. By doing this, we ensure that the final movement of the gun will be out towards the target, where our arms will bio-mechanically lock automatically. It should be noted here, that while your arms may not get to a point of being "fully extended," extending as far as your range of motion allows while wearing heavy body armor or some other device or clothing across your chest accomplishes the same goal. "All the way out," is all the way out, regardless of whether your arms are perfectly straight or not... the trick is to only move your arms in one direction at the end the presentation: Out towards the threat.

If the final movement of the gun is a swinging motion (up or to the side) instead of an outward movement towards the threat to a bio-mechanical stopping point, there will be momentum that must be stopped with muscular action. *Inertia* is the propensity of a body in motion (the gun in your hand) to remain in motion until acted upon by an opposing force. Inertia creates deviation which means that you'll have to slow down your response for more precise shooting by swinging your gun into position as opposed to extending it. As Colonel Rex Applegate notes in *Kill or Get Killed,*

> "It will be apparent that it is very difficult to swing your arm horizontally in a new direction and stop it in time to obtain the proper windage for accurate firing. this is especially true in combat. Ordinarily, two-thirds of the shots will be fired at the target either before the weapon reaches it or after it has passed across it and is on the other side. You can't make your

arm stop in the same place twice without excessive practice."
(Applegate, 1976)

The observations that Col. Applegate makes are consistent with all modern empirical evidence and the way the body works. If you haven't read his book, published 30 years ago, you should.

Grip & Trigger Control

Gripping the gun is also very simple... hold the gun with your strong hand as high as you can without interfering with the operation of the slide or risking injury to yourself. Your strong hand thumb should be high on the grip, not wrapped around so that it makes contact with the middle finger. This will create a gap that the thumb and the base of the palm of the weak hand can fit into. The fingers of the weak hand should be wrapped around the front of the grip, on top of and parallel to the strong hand fingers. Ensure that your thumbs are not crossed, but rather layered, with the strong thumb on top of the weak thumb.

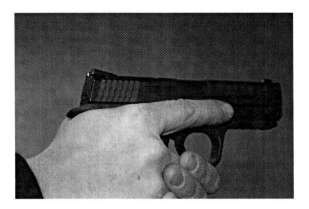

This grip works for 98% of the shooters I've seen with typical defensive handguns. If it doesn't work perfectly for you, try to keep as many components as possible and experiment until you find something comfortable and functional.

In a two handed grip, the fingers of the weak hand should be parallel with the fingers of the strong hand on the front of the grip area. Note the position of the trigger finger on the frame of the pistol, where it should remain until the shooter is ready to shoot.

Layering the thumbs is incredibly important to maintaining as good a two handed grip as possible. Crossing the thumbs in any way pulls or pushes some part of your hands away from the grip area of the firearm.

Trigger Control is all about contact and pressure. When I teach a new shooter or an advanced unorthodox shooting technique, shooting always starts with the actual trigger touching being split into two steps: Touch & Press. Separating these two for the former group is a matter of control; for the latter, it is usually a safety issue. You have better control over the trigger if you think of the action of pulling the trigger as a two step process from the point where your finger comes off the safe position against the frame. Touching the trigger is very different from pressing the trigger. Obviously, most shooters should quickly progress to the point where this becomes a subconscious separation, but learning it and thinking about it as a two step process is an important fundamental.

The one handed version of this grip is exactly the same for the strong hand, the thumb should still remain high on the weak side of the grip.

The number one way to tighten rapid fire groups for most shooters is to focus on the contact of the trigger finger during these strings of fire. This must be trained so that it becomes automatic. Once the commitment is made to touch the trigger at the beginning of a string of fire, the shooter's finger should not leave the trigger until the entire string of fire is complete.

The next most common error in this area is for the shooter to allow the trigger to travel much further forward than is necessary for the operation of the firearm. Finding the minimal forward travel distance (the "reset point") is something that you must do for each firearm that you shoot. That being said, if you shoot firearms that have radically different trigger reset points, you could be setting yourself up for failure during a critical incident if you "short stroke" the trigger by not allowing it to move forward enough after practicing with a very short reset gun, such as a single action semi-automatic pistol.

I am firm believer that a good defensive shooter and skilled weapons handler should be able to use any common type of firearm, but it is incredibly important to practice realistically with the gun and gear that you actually intend to use to defend yourself as often as possible.

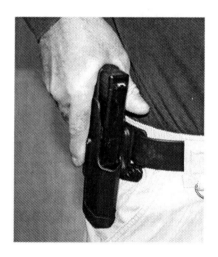

Presentation from the Holster

Presentation from the holster starts with the recognition of the threat and follows the same basic principles discussed in the previous sections. After achieving as much of a good firing grip as possible, the gun should be brought up out of the holster, oriented towards the threat and then extended through the ready position, with the presentation finishing exactly as described previously.

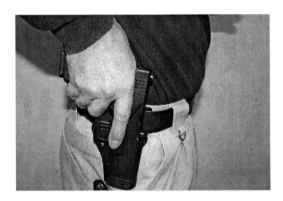

The details of the instructions given below are for strong side, hip or thigh holster configurations. While other carry methods may be suitable for special situations, they are not the best choice for 98% of the people 98% of the time. Those other methods will have specific variations to this technique and should be considered part of advanced training.

Combat Focus Shooting

Achieving a Good Firing Grip

If you are using a good defensive holster, you should be able to achieve 95+% of this grip before the gun starts its upward movement from the holster. At the same time that you attain this grip, you must defeat any mechanical retention devices that are inherent to the holster. Whether this means unsnapping something, twisting the gun, rolling a hood or pushing a button, it should be done efficiently and consistently as soon as you make contact with the gun, in the process of attaining your firing grip.

This position, the gun in a good firing grip with any holster retention defeated, but the gun still in the holster, is called "staged". While this position is not one that we often see used in training, it is one that both armed professionals and defensive shooters often find themselves in during the beginning stages of what might become a dynamic critical incident."

Consequently, choosing a retention holster with devices that are deactivated as efficiently as possible is important. Holsters like the G-Code SOC-Rig and BlackHawk SERPA holsters are examples of such holsters. Many holsters require actions that are incongruous with efficiently achieving a good firing grip. Ultimately, Weapon Retention should be an awareness and training issue, not a gear issue. Your holster should keep your gun safely contained and controlled during your normal activities, *you* must protect it from being taken away during a critical incident and be able to use it as quickly as possible when necessary.

Pull the Gun *Up*

The next step is to pull the gun straight up out of the holster against your body. Keeping the gun against your body at this point aids in retention and ensures that the gun will be extended *out* through the ready position towards the target, not swung.

Orient the Gun Towards the Threat

This step is crucial in the consistent alignment of the gun with your line of sight. It is also important *not* to articulate this as "pointing the gun towards the front," as there may come in your advanced training, or during a real critical incident, that you will be orienting the gun towards a threat in a direction other than your front!

The picture to left shows the firearm during extension, note that it is already parallel with the line of sight.

Extend the Gun Through the Ready Position

It is at this point that you will attain your two handed grip, if appropriate, and get the gun into and parallel with your line of sight and then complete the presentation of the firearm *out* towards the threat.

Keep in mind that you will be constantly assessing the threat during this process, able to stop at any point and keep the gun in the holster or at the High Compressed Ready Position if it is not necessary to shoot. The gun should not be extended past the ready if you do not intend to shoot!

Fundamental Combat Focus Shooting Drills

I was asked by a student in a class of would-be Combat Focus Shooting Instructors, whether or not the basic Combat Focus Shooting course outline assumed that the students already had a basic knowledge of shooting fundamentals. The student, Dan Pauley, is an accomplished instructor of both tactics and martial arts and was serving as a Sergeant with the Telluride Marshal's Office. The Marshal's office is the primary law enforcement agency in Telluride, Colorado and a sister agency to the San Miguel County Sheriff's Office, where I serve as a Training Officer. Although I knew that Dan, a long time police officer and pistol enthusiast, was asking about such things as sight alignment and sight picture, I responded with the fundamentals of shooting as I saw them: "The fundamentals of shooting are: "Look at the target; extend, touch, press".

Dan, who had been training with me at The Valhalla Training Center as part of a recurring Tactical Refresher program with his agency for about 3 years prior to attending the Instructor Development class, understood what I meant. He was certified during that class and now, in addition to teaching occasionally at Valhalla, integrates Combat Focus fundamentals and concepts into his training elsewhere. A major part of his, and any Combat Focus Shooting Instructor's integration, is the use of specific drills with shooters at all skill levels to help them develop Efficiency, Consistency and a good understanding of their personal Balance of Speed

& Precision. Many of these drills are being presented here for you to utilize on your own or with others.

Over the past two decades, I've seen a lot of great drills and a lot of not so great ones. While Combat Focus is not an unsighted only shooting program, it stresses that shooters need to understand when to use the sights and when not too. The Extend, Touch, Press! and Up! Drills, for example, need to be set up so that shooters are engaging a realistically sized target area simulating the High Center Chest at a distance of 7-10 feet. I've yet to see a student that couldn't consistently get hits under those conditions with unsighted fire. After you have developed a comfort with both appropriate unsighted and sighted fire, you will begin the process of developing an intuitive recognition of which is the best choice under a given circumstance. The first step of that development is, of course, shooting under a variety of conditions (the more realistic the better) to experience for yourself what your personal Balance of Speed & Precision is for any number of given circumstances. As noted earlier, an instructor cannot answer the "at what distance/size/situation should I use my sights", with any answer other than "When you need them". Understanding when that is requires realistic training and is part of being a Warrior Expert. These Balance of Speed & Precision Drills are great places to start creating templates for your Warrior Expert mind.

While using them, remember the tenets of Safety, Comfort and Competency!

Extend, Touch, Press! & Up!

The most basic fundamental drills in Combat Focus Shooting are the "Extend, Touch, Press" (ETP) and "Up!" Drills. As noted throughout this book, the basics of defensive shooting are not about firearms terminology, weapons maintenance, stance, the law or many of the other things that students are often taught prior to actually putting holes in paper. The basics are recognizing the threat and responding appropriately by getting combat accurate hits: "Look at the target; extend, touch, press." These two drills drive that point home for all shooters, from the newest to the most experienced. With the ETP drill, the only goal is to impart to the shooter an understanding of the three separate steps of final presentation towards the target and the firing of a round. Through this drill, you can achieve and practice proper trigger control, grip and presentation. You want to make sure that your stance is consistent with a plausible position during a dynamic critical incident (lowered center of gravity, weight forward, generally squared off towards the target, etc.). Using this drill as a warm-up with another shooter acting as range officer is a great idea. When doing so, it is imperative that shooters hold their shots until the "press" command in order to get the most out of the drill. Do not be tempted to just go ahead and shoot on your own.

This drill is performed at a realistic critical incident distance from the target; 7-10 feet is a good place to practice most defensive shooting drills.

At this range, remember to focus on the target, not any part of the gun and to keep the gun in your line of sight. You'll probably find pretty quickly that you can lower the gun out of your line of sight and still achieve combat accurate hits. Doing so would be counter productive... consistency is paramount. Keep the gun in the same place relative to your head.

Some Things to Look for:

If your handgun is moving after extension and before the shot, you are not presenting properly and/or you are probably looking at the gun/sights. Most of the time that the shooter moves the gun around after it is fully extended, it is because they are looking at the gun.

Be sure not to "cheat yourself"... The truth is that at the pace you will be moving, there is no penalty in efficiency for looking at the sights and they do increase accuracy. This is why it is very important to stress that all hits in the accepted Combat Accurate area are equal at the beginning of the drill. Furthermore, as the realism of the conditions and pacing increases, you'll be more interested in shooting faster and you will want to have established comfort with the concept of unsighted fire now.

After you are consistently getting Combat Accurate hits with ETP, you should switch to one single command (I usually use the word "Up!," which is how the drill got its name) for all three actions. When the command is given (or you think it to yourself) you might even go slower than during ETP the first few times, until you feel comfortable speeding up.

Once you are getting hits consistently within the Up! Drill, integrate lateral movement at the moment of command (which is simulating recognition of a threat).

The S-E-B Drill

The S-E-B Drill is named after the Law Enforcement Target Company's SEB target. This target has two large boxes and a triangle inside the gray bowling pin shaped silhouette and a series of small shapes containing the numbers 1 through 6 spaced around it. This is the same target the we use for the ETP and Up! Drills at The Valhalla Training Center, using the large square in the high center chest area to represent the Combat Accurate hit area. In the S-E-B Drill, it is again best to have a training partner to issue commands. The person calling should alternate calls between "Up!" and one of the numbers ("Two!" for example). The shapes are significantly smaller than the box in the chest of the target, so the shooter will get to experience the difference in the speed with which they can get consistent hits at the given distance between two different size targets. There is also a factor of predictability of the target slowing response to the number targets. The effect of this factor is increased if the "Up!" command is called significantly more often (twice as often or more) than a number.

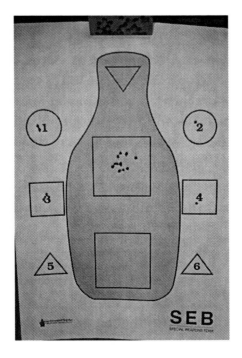

The tight groups on the target above would be applauded on most target ranges. If the assumption is that the center box and outer shapes represent the Combat Accurate hit areas, then from a Combat Focus Shooting point of view, they probably indicate that the shooter is shooting too slowly.

Some Things to Look for:

Some shooters will have a tendency to try to shoot the smaller, less predictable targets as fast as they shoot the large box. If you are consistently missing, slow down.... On the other hand, if you are consistently hitting, but shooting at the same speed, you can probably hit the center box faster!

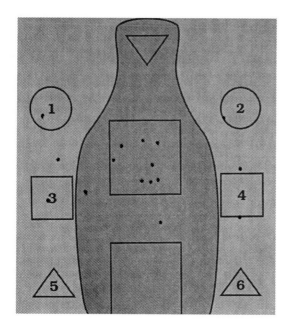

The target at left shows that the shooter is either not using good fundamentals or is shooting too fast for his ability at the given range. Without seeing the shooter in action, there is no way to tell.

Colored Numbers

The Colored Number Drill is named after Law Enforcement Target company's target number DT-2C, which has six small targets on it, each with a number 1 through 6. The targets are a mix of two squares, two circles and two triangles, all of which are roughly the same size. In this drill, also designed to let a shooter develop an understanding of their personal Balance of Speed & Precision, you can experience the effect of distance. Your training partner should call four of the six numbers about an equal number of times from a standard distance (6-8 feet) and then have you move back to about double the distance and call the other two numbers a few times each. To make the most of this drill , you should not be pushing your limits, but trying to attain 100% Combat Accurate hits. You can then compare and contrast your performance from the two ranges in terms of number of misses or tightness of groups in either series of targets.

For all of the example pictures in this section, assume that the 3 and 4 targets were shot from the further distance.

Some Things to Look for:

Be aware that an overly tight group from either range indicates that you are shooting too slowly! Any shot that hits the target area in this drill is equal (Combat Accurate).

Often, while evaluating student's targets, I see targets with fewer misses from the longer distances because shooters tend to try harder when they get further away or are over-confident when they are close (pesky human behavior!).

The target at left shows a good Balance of Speed & Precision. For this and all of the other Colored Number Drill pictures, assume that the 6, 1, 5 and 2 were all shot from the close distance and that the 3 and 4 were shot from the farther range.

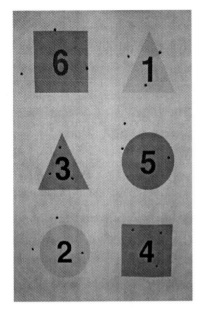 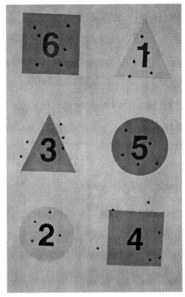

This target shows good hits on the 3 and 4, the far targets, but shooting that, if all the fundamentals were in place, was probably too fast at the close range targets.

The target at right is typical of a shooter who needs to understand that the Balance of Speed & Precision requires that they slow down for the further range targets (3 and 4).

Volume of Fire

The Volume of Fire Drills are any type of drill that require the shooter to shoot an undetermined number of rounds into a reactive target rapidly in order to cause it to go down. The most basic example is a steel popper target set leaning forward so that quick multiple shots are required to knock it down. In order to properly be a "Volume of Fire" drill, the target must be set so that multiple perfect hits fired *slowly* will never take the target down. By shooting these drills, you will be forced to fire rapid follow-up shots on a reasonably sized target at a realistic distance, while assessing the target.

Some Things to Look for:

Shooters will sometimes just shoot faster when they start missing instead of refining their fundamentals to try to get the target to go down. This doesn't work.

Keep in mind that you should be assessing the target constantly, shots fired *after* the target is going down are not good.

Cognitive Drills

"Cognitive Drills" are what I call the shooting drills that require the shooter to concentrate on something other than the shooting. Typically, I will use a pattern of shots that the student must fire into a sequence of targets as the distraction on a square range.

As an example: Load six rounds into two magazines and leave your weapon with a round chambered. After inserting the first magazine, you will be left with seven rounds in the gun and six in your reload. You should then be given (or give yourself) one command to initiate a complex sequence of fire. The sequence in this case might be 1 round to the abdomen, 2 to the chest, 1 to the head, 1 to the chest, 3 to the chest and then 5 to the chest. You should bring the gun into the ready position and execute lateral movement between each string of fire and during your reload. This leaves most students with a lot to think about other than just the shooting. You should try to execute the complete sequence "as fast as possible", pushing yourself to get combat accurate hits quickly. Shooters who follow the sequence properly and complete the sequence quickly while managing to get all the rounds in the appropriate areas have successfully reached the point of Balancing Speed & Precision in the context of a more realistic situation. This type of drill focuses on the idea that Combat Focus Shooting does not teach skills in isolation, but demands that the shooting be intuitive in the face of many other distractions to the cognitive process.

Some Things to Look for:

This drill almost requires a training partner for evaluation. You should be able to figure out how many rounds should be in any given area of the target pretty easily, so that checking whether or not a shooter followed the directions can be done quickly.

Other key points to look for are the number of rounds shot to complete a string after a reload or to end the string.

Push Your Limit

The "Push Your Limit" Drill is one of the newest to be added to the Combat Focus curriculum. This drill was brought into the program by Valhalla's Operations Assistant, Brad Schuppan. He first saw it used as a drill to teach trigger control by another instructor. Brad recognized the drill's value to Combat Focus students and instructors as it forces students to shoot at a pace that, eventually, moves beyond their Balance of Speed & Precision. I have seen no better drill to quickly ensure that a student is pushing himself to the edge. The shooter should stand 5-7 feet from any target with multiple small target areas of similar size. Generally, I use the small shapes on the ubiquitous SEB target. On the first shape, the shooter should count, out loud, "One-one-thousand, Two-one-thousand," etc., up to "Five," firing a round on each new number. This results in about 1 round per second.

Next, the shooter should count "One and Two and Three and Four and Five" again, firing a round on each new number. The result is five shots with about 1/2 second in between each.

The next step in the drill is for the shooter to count "1,2,3,4,5," as fast as they can, again firing at each new number. The result is five shots in about a second or slightly longer.

The shooter can now look over the results of the faster shots. If you managed to keep all five shots of the last string in the target, the next step is to take one full pace backwards and repeat the final string of fire. That process can be repeated until the you are pushed beyond your limit. This drill can be used as a continuing measure of increased competency.

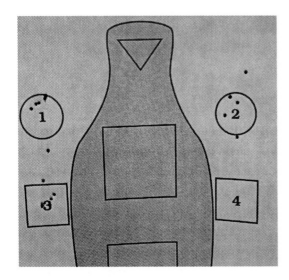

The upper target shows that the shooter is either shooting beyond their ability in the sec-ond and third section of the drill or, more likely, not using good fundamentals.

The lower target shows a more typical performance at 5-7 feet from a shooter using good fundamentals.

Figure 8 Drill

The most important drill that I use for advanced training on a square range is the Figure 8 Drill. This drill was shown to me in the mid-nineties by Hector Martinez. "Marty" had recently gotten out of the military, where he had been running firearms training at the PSD School at Fort McClellan. That school is now taught at Fort Leavenworth, but at the time Marty was there, as a Marine, he worked with an outstanding cadre from all branches of the US Military. Marty and I were introduced through a mutual acquaintance in the private security industry in Nashville. With a mutual interest in training beyond the level of tight groups, we instantly hit it off. Over the course of the next 5 years, most of our time together was spent working in the security industry, talking about training or actually out on the range. One afternoon at the range, Marty threw a couple of empty ammo boxes on the ground about 10-15 feet from the target stands and had me walk in a Figure 8 around them. He then called "Up!" and I would turn towards the targets and engage appropriately. For years I used this drill sparingly, usually with more advanced students to teach reaction in 360 degrees.

It wasn't until I had the 360-degree ranges at The Valhalla Training Center that I realized the incredible power of the Figure 8 drill. With the Figure 8, anyone with a traditional square range could safely move a huge leap towards Valhalla-like range conditions with the right set-up and thought process.

I use the Figure 8 drill in all aspects of training to test skills in 360 degrees. Whether we are looking at holster presentation, target identification, executive protection, low-light tactics, multiple shooters or just about any other skill you can imagine, there is a way to integrate the Figure 8 Drill. Rarely do I teach a shooting class that someone doesn't comment at the end about how they can't wait to share the Figure 8 drill with their unit, agency, students or shooting buddies.

The easiest way to set up an entry level Figure 8 Drill is to put up a single silhouette type target about 10 feet from the two marks that the shooter is going to walk around and use any firing command. To make things more interesting, you might trying shooting one of the other drills in this section in the Figure 8 format, such as the SEB Drill.

The next step is to use multiple targets with numbers spray painted on them, using the numbers as the firing commands. At first, the numbers should be different. As the drill moves on, additional targets can be added and numbers can be duplicated to test multiple target responses. Alternatively, instead of using numbers, different types of realistic silhouettes can be used and corresponding one-word descriptions (such as shirt colors) can be the target calls, instead of numbers. If resources and range safety allow, targets can be set up staggered from the Figure 8 line, to create bystanders and obstructions to clear shots on some targets. Similarly, reactive three-dimensional targets or steel can also be used. Keep in mind that during this drill, which should only be used once one is comfortable and confident with presentation from the holster. The shooter must *recognize* the threat and orient

Combat Focus Shooting

towards it before presenting the gun from the holster, but the grip may be attained during this movement prior to the gun coming up out of the holster. Shooters can be kept honest by occasionally having non-existent targets called (a "Five!" when there is no target with a "5" on it, for example) to represent "no-shoots".

This drill requires at least one training partner to be used efficiently and safely.

Bonus Chapter: Choosing a Defensive Handgun

All handguns are a compromise. How you choose to compromise is often as much a result of your circumstances as it is your preferences or beliefs. If you live in Alaska, you have more options during most of the year than you do if you live in Miami. If you weigh 160 pounds and work in an office setting, you have fewer options than someone who shops in the big & tall section and works in the outdoors.

The compromises between a modern "Safe-Action" type weapon such as the Glock, a traditional double/single action semi-auto and the ubiquitous single action pistols are numerous. I strongly believe that the simplicity in the use and instruction of the modern designs such as the Glock family of pistols, the Springfield XD and the Smith & Wesson M&P offer huge advantages in a combative pistol. Pull the trigger and they go "bang!"… the same way every time. No de-cocking, no separately operated external safety. Finger off the trigger and you're in the safe mode. After more than two decades in service in the United States, this type of design has proven itself. Of course, like any design type, there have been poor examples, but there are many more successful ones. The increased safety of the long, heavy, first shot double-action guns come with little other benefit and the burden of two different trigger pulls and the need to de-cock after firing. The single action designs at least offer a much crisper and shorter trigger pull to be weighed against the need to manually operate the safety lever prior to and after shooting.

Regardless of the way the statistics are collected or spun, the area of the body the bullet strikes is infinitely more important than the difference between any major defensive/combative pistol caliber from 9mm to .45acp. When students ask me for a caliber recommendation, I simply say that you should carry the largest weapon of the type you prefer and carry as conveniently as you need to. Then choose that weapon in the largest caliber that you can shoot well. That means if their circumstances dictate that you can only carry a small flat "sub-caliber" semi-auto, you'll probably choose a .32 over a .25. If you are considering a .380, you can probably find a small 9mm in the same size and weight range. If you like the Glock 19, you might find that you can handle the Glock 23 and trade 2 rounds of capacity for the extra energy of the .40 S&W round in the same size package. If you prefer single action automatics, the choice of size and caliber still exists.

Of course, I can't leave this topic without pointing out that a small frame .38 special revolver may be the best bet for your defensive needs and a full size .357 or .45 revolver the perfect choice for home defense. Lately, I'm much more likely to have a J-frame .38 in a pocket holster than any other defensive weapon. Not as sexy as the semi-auto and certainly not as capable as a combative weapon, the convenience of carry and reliability of revolvers are hard to beat for low-threat condition defensive tools.

There is something to be said for style choice also. Going armed is usually either a professional or lifestyle choice. In both realms, we must acknowledge the factor of style. As noted earlier in the book, a individual's comfort has a lot to do with their progress in training and their judgment about when to pull the trigger. It may not sound very practical, but I do believe that if you like your gun, you are going to shoot it more often, train more seriously. When I was issued a double action only H&K USP, I didn't train nearly as much with it as I did when my duty gun was a Beretta 92. If anything, I was training and shooting more during the USP era, but I can admit that I was not training with my duty gun as much because I didn't prefer it. So, as far as style goes, I say that if it doesn't cause a compromise in reliability, weight, comfort, caliber or accuracy, carry the version of pistol that makes you happy. As long as you can shoot it well and carry it conveniently, let your friend's snicker at the tiger striped stainless/blued Browning High Power if they want.

Acknowledgments

This book, in fact, the entire Combat Focus Shooting Program, would not exist if it were not for the assistance, support, questioning, challenging, enthusiasm, inquiring, trust, dedication tolerance and/or patience of *many* people. In preparing to write this section, I realized quickly that not everyone can be named, but a few need to be.

As noted in the main body, Combat Focus Shooting, the codification of the program, basic course curriculum and the instructor development process have only come about at this time because of my position as the Director of Operations at The Valhalla Shooting Club & Training Center and the relationship that I have with the owner, Tom Forman. Tom Forman originally built the building that is now Valhalla as a recreational amenity for the world-class Elk Mountain Resort. He often says that after 9-11, while the larger resort project was still being developed, he realized that there could be a training component to the site. The truth is that Tom has been teaching martial arts, self-defense and shooting skills to people for almost 2 decades and would certainly have been using the facility for such endeavors with or without 9-11. In the fall of 2002, while evaluating Executive Security International's shooting program, I had the good fortune of meeting Tom and seeing the shooting ranges he had built. Approximately six months later he offered me a position as the director of his shooting club. Within four months of that discussion, I was living in Colorado and The Valhalla Shooting Club & Training Center was open for business. I had no idea then how far this endeavor would go so quickly. I also had no idea how much trust, support and friendship would come from Tom & Doris (his wife and partner), which is what has made everything that Valhalla has achieved possible.

Valhalla Training Center's owner, Tom Forman (Right), presenting the author with his Valhalla Member's Pistol in 2003.

In October of 1998 I received an email from someone I did not know inviting me to participate in an online firearms discussion forum. At the time, I was posting occasionally on the venerable rec. guns, often banging my head against a wall of internet commando lore and legend. The email came from Rich Lucibella and the forum he started that month was *The Firing Line*. That invitation was a fateful one, to which I owe an incredible amount of good fortune. From the development of *The Firing Line* community, through countless other endeavors related to the shooting industry, including Rich's acquisition of *S.W.A.T. Magazine* in 2001, Rich has invited me to participate where I could or agreed to help when I needed it. When he allowed me to join the staff of his magazine in 2001, my focus on becoming a leader in the tactical training community was galvanized. Rich's counsel has both pointed out when I've been wrong and helped me to be right. Over the past 8 years, Rich has become a Brother and demonstrated his support in too many ways, personally and professionally, to list.

The author with Rich Lucibella
in 2004

In 2001, I had the good fortune to become exposed to Tony Blauer
and the S.P.E.A.R. System™. Tony has studied human automatic
responses for over 20 years and has developed a variety of combative
training programs intrinsically bound to them. S.P.E.A.R. (Spon-
taneous Protection Enabling an Accelerated Response), is *the*
pre-eminent unarmed counter-ambush combatives program available to warriors today because of this fact. 90% of the research
that I have done into the physiological and neuroscientific aspects
of The Combat Focus Shooting Program are directly related to or
inspired by Tony's programs and research in these areas. Tony is
the most dynamic and articulate instructor in the industry. He is
a dedicated friend and family man. Tony has been very generous
and trusting in allowing me to utilize his research in dozens of
articles, on television, in training programs and, obviously, this
book. The fact is that he wants to collect & create information that
makes people safer... and wants, more passionately than anyone I
know, to share his information with the people who need it.

S.P.E.A.R. Instructor Course, 2001

The Staff at The Valhalla Training Center over the past 3 years has, under a variety of conditions, truly made the actual writing of this book possible. Brad Schuppan and Jeremiah Miles, particularly, have spent an incredible amount of time teaching courses while I was typing paragraphs and sending emails. Furthermore, their intellectual contributions to the integrity of the system through constantly pushing the program forward and their dedication to making our students more dangerous has taken Combat Focus Shooting to new levels. Of Course, without Nicole, Corey and the many support staff from Elk Mountain Resort keeping things running in the background, the instructor staff wouldn't be able to teach anyone.

It should go without saying, but must be mentioned, that any and all of my instructors over the years in a myriad of endeavors are actually the ones who are responsible for a great deal of the information in this book. Whether by example, anecdote, experience or articulation they have all added something to my professional development.

Valhalla Training Center Staff & Adjuncts, Military Special Operations Course, Nov 2006: Back: John Brown (A), Kent O'Donnell (A), Brad Schuppan (S), Nicole Mata (S), Robert Rock (A). Front: Rob Pincus (S), David Breed (A), Scott Berendes (A), Jeremiah Miles (S), Corey Eschelman (S). Not Pictured: Tom Forman (S), Dan Pauley (A), Skip Batley (A)

The first SHOT Show that I attended was in 1997. Over the past 10 years I have made some great friends in the training, shooting & hunting industries. Their support in a variety of endeavors has been invaluable. It would be impossible to list everyone, but Denny Hansen, Ken Jorgensen, Alan Brosnan, Clint & Heidi Smith, Greg Chevalier, (and staff...) Melinda Calnan, Chuck Fretwell, Ashley Emerson, Holden Kris, Jack Robertson, Gary Meares, Bob Morrison, Tim Cameron, Joe Troiani, Col. Robert Brown, Michael Tull, Scott Evans, John Ross, Jim D'Elia and Joe Coury have all distinguished themselves over some period of time with their support.

The Certified Combat Focus Shooting Instructors across the country have all been an important part of this process. Mike Westcott, Tony Namio, John Brown and Kent O'Donnell have also been instrumental in spreading the program.

The author's favorite student, Christina Pincus

It is perhaps most important, however, that I thank my students. Whether at a MOUT site in Florida, a dirt berm in Tennessee, a coral reef in The Keys, an underground range in Munich or the most advanced 360 degree live fire range in the world at Valhalla, anyone who ever took the time, the chance and/or the effort to let me try to share something with them receives my sincere gratitude and acknowledgment for helping me to become a better teacher. By having read this book, you are now included in this list.

Finally, the actual preparation of this book has been directly supported by several people not listed above, but deserving of mention: My Mom, my Dad, Mykl Spencer, Jeremiah Miles, David Breed, Robert Smith, Shanna Frey and Dennis Samuel actually took time to proof-read and spot-check the entire manuscript. Betty Shonts delivered outstanding cover design and interior illustrations on short notice. Of course, Robert Smith also provided the outstanding Reading List and Commentary in Appendix 2.

Thanks,

Rob Pincus, December 2nd, 2006

(vscrob@msn.com)

Appendix 1: Glossary of Important Terms

Cognitive –

Cognitive Processing is necessary to make decisions, which takes time and effort. Pre-Cognitive reactions occur within the brain at the time of recognition of a threat, we do not need decide to flinch or to initiate "tunnel vision," for example.

Combat Accuracy –

(also "Defensive Accuracy" when appropriate)Any shot that significantly effects our target to present a lethal threat.

Comfort-

You must be intellectually and physically comfortable with concepts and skills if they are going to become competent with them. Students must be encouraged to ask questions and voice concerns so that an Instructor may address them. In formal training, comfort is the shared responsibility of the Instructor and the Student.

Competency –

Competency is the final goal of all training sessions. Competency is an individual subjective measurement and should not be quantified objectively or capped.

Consistency -

Consistency (especially in physical skills) increases efficiency. The fewer options a student has for dealing with a certain situation or problem, the more consistent their response will be.

Deviation -

Deviation during shooting is the amount of variance between the alignment of the firearm and our line of sight to the target. Deviation can be introduced by a variety of factors, such as: trigger pull, body motion, movement of the target, etc.

Dynamic Critical Incident

Any uncontrolled situation which involves or requires the use of or serious threat of violent lethal force.

Effectiveness -

Achieving our stated goal without regard for the means used to achieve it.

Efficiency -

Using as little time, effort and/or energy as possible. Efficiency in achieving our stated goal from a known or predictable starting point is what the CF Shooting program is all about. Efficiency includes EFFECTIVENESS.

Expert –

We want to be Warrior Experts. Experts process information differently than layman. An expert compares incoming information to a known set of templates and uses those templates to speed the decision making process to an appropriate response. The more realistically our students train, the more likely it is that they have a template in their head that is appropriate to their Dynamic Critical Incident.

Intuitive -

We use the word "intuitive" to describe the way we integrate with the environment, conditions and tools that we use during a critical incident when we are maximizing our EFFICIENCY. Intuitive responses require less COGNITIVE process and encourage CONSISTENCY.

Safety-

In training, the potential risks of any drill, session, etc must be SIGNIFICANTLY outweighed by the perceived benefits of those endeavors. Safety is the responsibility of the instructors and range staff.

Significantly –

Whenever possible, we want our actions during a Dynamic Critical Incident to significantly effect our threat's ability to harm us or someone else.

Appendix 2: Human Weapon System Reading List

Robert C. Smith, M.D., Direct Action Medical Network

www.directactionmedicalnetwork.com

"Employ your time in improving yourself by other men's writings, so that you shall gain easily what others have labored hard for."

—Socrates

The list of references in this Appendix represent books that should be read more than once if you make your living fighting or training people to fight. Collectively they form the basis for much of what is taught in Combat Focus Shooting. Taken globally they are the foundational material on which the principles stand. The first time I was at Valhalla I found a synergy of thought that was summed up in the term Warrior/Scholar.

Warrior/Scholars spend time studying how and why approaches and themes of fighting work or fail, regardless of the source. This is done with a humble confidence that comes from trusting that "truth stands the test of time." There are other sources of information. I am sure that you have favorites that you would willingly fight about. What is important is that a person has the perspective that humans have dominated the planet because of their ability to adapt and utilize tools. Humans are Weapon Systems and like all weapon systems they can be put to good use or evil. In his book <u>How to Read a Book</u> Mortimer Adler describes how to read different kinds of subject matter material. When it comes to medical textbooks go slow, look at diagrams and tables find things that make sense and start with those. Overtime you will acquire vocabulary and a sense of what an incredible HWS you posses. This knowledge overtime will lead to more effective training and less fear about injury and pain.

Combat Focus Shooting is on track. It makes physiologic and anatomic sense. Tony Blauer's S.P.E. A. R. System is on track. It makes physiological and anatomical sense. The reason both of these systems work, is, they are based on utilizing the structure and nature of humans to dominate the fight. The Human Weapon System is complex, but worthy of study for a lifetime.

DAMN Reading List

A War Like No Other, Victor Davis Hanson

An Autumn of War, Victor Davis Hanson

Atlas of Human Anatomy, 3rd Ed, Frank H. Netter

Gates of Fire, Steven Pressfield

On Guerilla Warfare, Mao Tse-Tung

Imperial Grunts, Robert Kaplan

Proverbs, Solomon

On Intelligence, Jeff Hawkins

On Killing, David Grossman

Ripples of Battle, Victor Davis Hanson

The Art of War, Sun Tzu

The Ultimate Terrorist, Jessica Stern

Textbook of Medical Physiology, C. Guyton

"You can tell a lot about a man by listening to him talk to God and looking at what he reads." — Paul C. Smith DVM

Bibliography

Applegate, R. (1976). *Kill or Get Killed*. Boulder, CO: Paladin Press.

Doss, W. (2003). *Train to Win*. Bloomington, IN: 1stBooks (now Authorhouse).

Hawking, S. (1993). *Black Holes and Baby Universes*. New York, NY: Bantam Books.

Hawkins, J. (2004). On Thinking. New York, NY: Henry Holt & Company.

Geary, D. (2005). *The Origin of Mind*. Washington, DC: American Psychological Association.

Greene, R. (2006). *33 Strategies of War*. New York, NY: Penguin Group.

Little, J. (Ed.). (1997). *Jeet Kune Do*. North Clarendon, VT: Tuttle Publishing.

Murray, K. (2004). *Training at the Speed of Life*. Gotha, FL: Armiger Publications.

Rauch, R. W. (1998). *Real World Survival*. Lafayette Hill, PA: Rauch & Company, LTD.

Ross. P. (2006) *The Expert Mind*, Scientific American, Vol 294, Iss 8: Scientific American, Inc.

Training Videos
NOW AVAILABLE

Combat Focus Shooting DVD

This exciting video brings the information and drills contained in the book to life with real time demonstrations and the latest insights on realistic firearms training and the Combat Focus Shooting Program from Rob Pincus.

Shooting in Realistic Environments

Combining the fundamentals of Combat Focus Shooting with practical advise about shooting in realistic situations and environments, this video covers target engagement areas, proper use of cover, the critical incident reload and several other topics. Taped during an actual course at The Valhalla Training Center, the video even follows students through runs in the unique 360 degree live fire ranges. Also featured are exclusive Private Lessons for the video students.

Visit www.valhallatraining.com to see our online store's complete selection of books, videos and logo clothing.

Coming Soon:

Combat Focus Shooting, Vol 2:

Advanced Weapons Handling & Tactics

-By Rob Pincus

Visit www.Valhallatraining.com and to learn more about Combat Focus Shooting, Valhalla's Training Programs, Rob Pincus and to join our Newsletter to keep up with the latest information and training opportunities.

Visit www.valhallatraining.com to see our
online store's complete selection of books, videos and logo clothing.

"All of our officers are trained in Combat Focus and we use it extensively…more often then not our range program is right in line with police combat and surviving violent attacks. We have also included it in our carbine course and so far have had the same positive response."

—Tony Namio, Law Enforcement Firearms Instructor, WI

"We are completing our second basic police academy class using the Combat Focus Shooting skills. Our cadets have qualified faster than ever before in both academy sessions."

—Kent O'Donnell, Training Officer, NM

"Since we started incorporating some of the Combat Focus techniques into the Deputy Sheriff's Basic Training Academy Firearms Program, we have been able to develop more efficient and effective shooters than ever before. As the Firearms Coordinator for this program, I am always looking for ways to improve shooter performance. The trip my staff and I made to Colorado was well worth it."

—Randy Smith, Firearms Instructor, PA

"Mr. Pincus has organized this thing and has described it as a training system, which can help save your life when the moment we all want to avoid comes."

—John Caradimis, The M1911 Pistols Organization, Greece

Combat Focus Shooting Courses and Instructor Development Training is available exclusively through the Valhalla Training Center in Montrose, Colorado. Courses can be conducted at Valhalla or on your range anywhere in the world.

Printed in the United States
146455LV00006B/171/A

9 780979 150869